The New York Times
COLLECTION

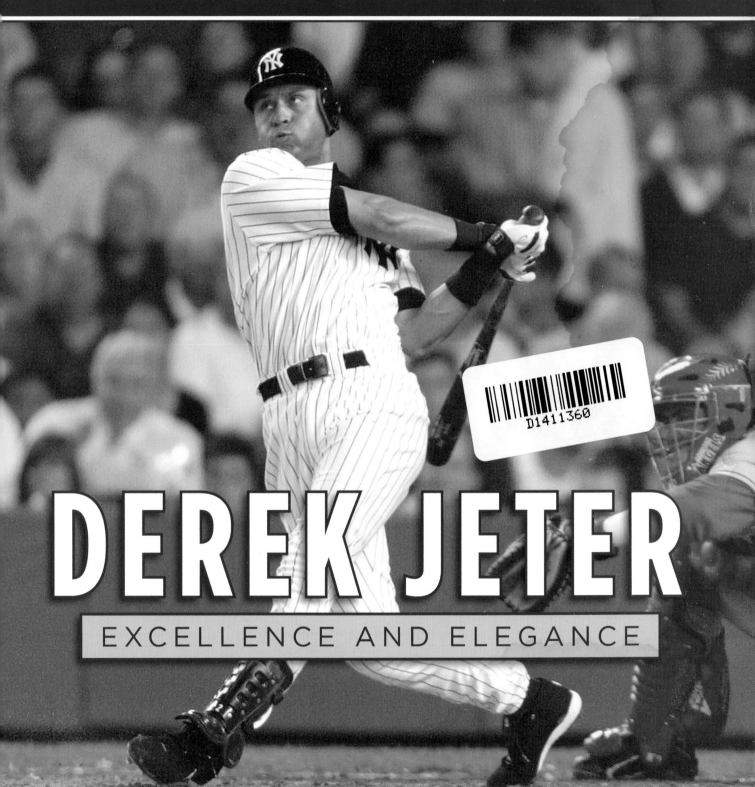

DEREK JETER
EXCELLENCE AND ELEGANCE

This book is available in quantity at special discounts for your group or organization.For further information, contact:

Triumph Books LLC
814 North Franklin Street
Chicago, Illinois 60610
Phone: (312) 337-0747
www.triumphbooks.com

Printed in U.S.A.
ISBN: 978-1-62937-052-1

The New York Times
Project Manager: Alex Ward
Photo Editor: Phyllis Collazo

Content packaged by Mojo Media, Inc.
Joe Funk: Editor
Jason Hinman: Creative Director

Front cover photo by Richard Perry/The New York Times
Back cover photo by Barton Silverman/The New York Times
Title page photo by Chang W. Lee/The New York Times

DONT BE SAD
ITS OVER....
BE GLAD
IT
HAPPENED ②

② LEGEND

LETSGO
JETER
FAREWELL
CAPTAIN RE2PECT

Barton Silverman/The New York Times

CONTENTS

Applause fills Yankee Stadium as Jeter steps from the dugout and teammates and fans alike stand to honor the Captain on Derek Jeter Day, September 7, 2014. (Barton Silverman/The New York Times)

Foreword

By Joe Torre

When I was hired as the manager of the New York Yankees on November 2, 1995, I knew that the organization had high hopes for a shortstop prospect who had spent most of the season at Triple-A Columbus. The Yankees felt strongly that a kid from Kalamazoo, Michigan could be a bona fide major league shortstop for a team with World Series dreams in 1996. I was grateful for the chance to manage the Yankees, and I trusted the team's judgment about Derek Jeter's readiness to be an everyday player for a winner. I just didn't know much about the young man.

Before our first spring training together, Derek helped me understand why the Yankees regarded him so highly. In a television interview that I happened to see, he was asked about taking over as the shortstop of the Yankees. In response, he simply said, "I'm going to get an opportunity to win the job." I loved the humility of his answer. It struck me then that he was mature beyond his years. Derek knew that if he performed well, everything else would take care of itself. He was all about accountability and respect, without any sense of entitlement.

I was fortunate to serve as Derek's manager for 12 memorable years. During that time, I watched a 21-year-old with great potential rise to become one of the best shortstops in the history of the game. He is one of the most well-rounded players I've ever seen, with a presence of mind that can't be taught. Derek's ability to stay calm and focused – especially in our biggest moments – always amazed me. Even when he was a rookie, New York City never overwhelmed Derek; in fact, the stage brought out the best in him. Early on in '96, I realized that he

was making a huge impression on our accomplished, veteran players.

When the leader of your team is always doing the right thing, everybody else notices. And when the leader of your team is willing to plant his face in cement in order to get an out, it transforms the level to which his teammates are willing to compete. Eventually, Derek's attitude was woven into the DNA of our team. There were times when our collective talent may not have been better than our competition, but our capacity to grind it out made all the difference. Derek was instrumental in setting that tone.

A perfect illustration of what drives Derek Jeter came on July 9, 2011, when he recorded the 3,000th hit of his career with a third inning home run. I was at Yankee Stadium as a fan, hoping to see the milestone myself. Derek didn't just join one of the game's greatest pantheons that day; he also went 5-for-5. His base hit in the eighth inning gave the Yankees a 5-4 lead, soon closed out by his buddy Mariano Rivera. When I saw Derek after the game, he cared more about the single that put his team in position to win than he did about the homer that

made him the 28th player in baseball history to reach 3,000 hits. If the Yankees hadn't won that day, Derek wouldn't have been able to take any satisfaction in a personal achievement. That mentality is what turned him into a five-time World Series Champion.

Throughout this season, it has been a pleasure to see all the fans throughout the game show their appreciation for Derek. Personally, I will remember him as the consummate professional and competitor, one who has never taken a wrong turn in his career. Derek has earned his stature as one of the best

ambassadors that the national pastime has ever had, and he has set a remarkable example for every kid who dreams of being a part of major league baseball.

Those Yankee pinstripes have been worn by players with names like Ruth, Gehrig, DiMaggio, Mantle and Berra. As he walks away from the game, Derek Jeter will now be mentioned among that row of legends forever. I couldn't be happier for such a special young man. Just like it was the stroke of midnight, with October turning to November, Derek got an opportunity, and he knocked it out of the park.

Jeter and Torre confer before a game. (Barton Silverman/The New York Times)

Introduction: Third Time's the Charm

By Tyler Kepner

We will remember the victories, of course. The inside-out singles to right, the leaping throws from the grass in shallow left, the way he always ran hard, no matter what. But as the years go by, what will resonate most about the breathtaking career of Derek Jeter is what he did not do.

He did not let us down.

Every great story needs a conflict, and there are plenty to be found in every baseball game. Jeter, after all, made more than 8,000 outs and more than 250 errors. Most of his seasons did not end with a championship.

But the controversies that leveled so many of his athletic peers did not trap Jeter. You could look to him and believe with confidence that he would not show up his opponents. He would not disparage his teammates. He would not leave for a better contract. He would not embarrass himself, his family or the Yankees, on or off the field. He would not cheat.

"If you were sitting two decades ago and you said, 'Boy, this is a guy that I want to be the face of baseball and be what this generation will remember, you couldn't have written a script like this,'" said Commissioner Bud Selig, on the day of Jeter's final All-Star Game in 2014. "How lucky can this sport be to have the icon of this generation turn out to be Derek Jeter? It's absolutely remarkable."

Jeter grew up in Kalamazoo, Mich., next to a baseball field. It was right there for him, just behind his backyard, beckoning him to play. He heeded the call for decades, through his 40th birthday, and with talent, drive and good fortune, he lived a dream.

Jeter was born in New Jersey, and he would visit his grandmother there in the summers. She was a Yankees fan, so he was, too. He was the best

high school player in the country his senior year, but five teams would be drafting ahead of his favorite. Remarkably, they all passed.

Jeter had a scholarship offer to the University of Michigan, and as the Yankees debated his merits, one official wondered aloud if Jeter would go to college. Dick Groch, the scout who would sign Jeter, responded with prescient words: "He's not going to Michigan. He's going to Cooperstown."

Groch was right, of course, and when Jeter gets there, he will not find many with a legacy as rich. At retirement, he ranked among the top 10 in major league history in hits and runs scored. Nobody started more games at shortstop. Among Yankees, nobody had more hits or played more games than Jeter, who won more titles in pinstripes than Babe Ruth.

Jeter's No. 2 will stand beside Ruth's No. 3 in the Yankees' numerical lineup, and it will seem perfectly at home. If the original Yankee Stadium was "The House That Ruth Built," the new one was made possible, largely, by Jeter. He was the linchpin of the teams that won four World Series from 1996 to 2000, catapulting the Yankees to a new stratosphere of riches, at the turnstiles and on television. Every empire needs a castle, and in 2009 Jeter helped christen the Yankees' palace with a championship in its very first season.

His performance dipped in 2010, his batting average tumbling 64 points. Jeter managed to

"How lucky can this sport be to have the icon of this generation turn out to be Derek Jeter?" said Commissioner Bud Selig. " It's absolutely remarkable."

score more runs—the only statistic that mattered to him, teammate Luis Sojo once mused—than he had the previous year, but negotiations on a new contract turned testy. Jeter never wanted to leave, he insisted, and was hurt that the Yankees publicly dared him to find a better offer.

He returned, of course, for a pay cut but still a handsome deal, and delivered in style. On a July afternoon in the Bronx, Jeter homered for his 3,000th hit—"History, with an exclamation point!" as Michael Kay called it, on the YES Network—and collected five hits in a victory.

"You knew he was going to do something special," reliever David Robertson reflected, a few years later. "And then just to hit a home run, it's like it was written to be."

Another playoff appearance followed, and in 2012, at age 38, Jeter led the majors in hits. His 216 were the most he had compiled in 13 years, but he ended the season crumpled on the dirt in October, felled by a broken ankle as he dove for a ball in the championship series.

"I was going to carry him in," said Joe Girardi, the manager, who rushed to Jeter's aid on the field. "He said, 'No—do not carry me.' That is the kind of guy he is."

Even at his weakest, most wounded moment, Jeter was true to himself. His season was over—and his next season all but ruined—but he had to win something, had to score some small victory. A proud competitor, he knew, walks off on his own.

That is how Jeter approached retirement, too. He called 2013 a nightmare, and while the candor seemed rare, he was only stating the obvious. Jeter played in just 17 games, shuffling to and from the disabled list, and the Yankees failed to reach the postseason for only the second time in his career. Before reporting to spring training the next February, Jeter announced on Facebook that the 2014 season would be his last.

It was his way of taking control over the one opponent no athlete can beat: age. Nobody plays forever, and Jeter, it turned out, did not want to. He wanted to explore more business and philanthropic work, he said. A celebrated bachelor, he said he hoped to start a family.

"And I want the ability to move at my own pace, see the world and finally have a summer vacation," he wrote.

Jeter said he had accomplished almost all of his goals and had no regrets. He would be celebrated throughout his final summer, with gifts and ceremonies and oversized checks to his foundation presented at every road ballpark he visited. He addressed the American League All-Star team—before getting two hits in the game—telling his teammates to savor every minute, because it goes by quickly.

"He just wanted to thank us," said Mike Trout, the young star for the Los Angeles Angels. "You know, we should be thanking him."

Trout was also born in New Jersey, and grew up admiring Jeter. Like Jeter he is genial and polite and multi-talented, an uncomplicated professional who seems to represent what is right in the game. Perhaps Trout can be an heir to Jeter as the icon of the game.

But in his time and town, to live the precise vision he had for himself, and to do it the way we hope we all would, if given the chance – there may never be another quite like Jeter. Wherever he goes from here, we can only hope that he lives out the words of Gene Wilder, from the final scene of "Willy Wonka and the Chocolate Factory," the children's fantasy movie.

"Don't forget what happened to the man who suddenly got everything he always wanted," said Wilder, as the title character.

"He lived happily ever after."

"He's more than just a baseball player," Mrs. Jeter proclaimed. "He's Derek."

Future Yankee Too Good to Be True?

By JACK CURRY • Published: August 26, 1994

Uncle Joe has skin cancer and it has spread. It is serious. Those were the only words Derek Jeter needed to hear from Aunt Julie before he used his first scheduled day off in six weeks to transform himself from a star shortstop in Columbus, Ohio, to a concerned nephew in Kearny, N.J.

Aunt Julie gave Derek a gold New York Yankees necklace when he was in the sixth grade and the gift helped form a strong bond between them. Necklace or not, Jeter did not need to be cajoled into spending Tuesday with Uncle Joe.

It was typical of Jeter, the Class AAA prospect who could be the starting shortstop for the Yankees next season if his fielding is deemed reliable. Finding fault with Jeter the player or the person is as arduous as finding interest in buying tickets for a Yankee game tonight.

"Joe had seen stories about Derek in the New York papers and said, 'I guess I'm not going to make it to see him play in Yankee Stadium,'" explained Dorothy Jeter, Derek's mother, her voice wavering during a telephone interview yesterday. "He said, 'I guess I won't ever get to see him.' So Julie told him, 'I'll bring him here.'"

She succeeded. After returning to Columbus that night, the 20-year-old Jeter called his mother in Kalamazoo, Mich.

"He said Joe didn't look good and it bothered him," Mrs. Jeter said. "I knew it would because he's never seen anybody sick. He said Uncle Joe was glad to see him. If Derek made him smile for 10 minutes, it was worth it."

If Jeter were an average college student who used a rare day off to journey three hours round trip to see an ill uncle, it would be a sweet story. But since Jeter is a former first-round draft pick who has catapulted from Class A to Class AAA in two months, who is being touted as a future All-Star and who has not changed from the pleasant kid who received that necklace eight years ago, it might be an even sweeter story.

"He's more than just a baseball player," Mrs. Jeter proclaimed. "He's Derek."

While that sounds like a boastful mother on her best day, it is not boasting when she

Jeter poses on the dugout steps at Yankee Stadium on Sept. 14, 1994, after being named *Baseball America's* minor league player of the year. (AP Photo/Mark Lennihan)

"I don't know what's going to happen," said Jeter. " They're going to do what they want to do. But I always knew the Yankees don't move people too quickly, so I was a little surprised when I came here."

is accurate. Manager Buck Showalter of the Yankees studied Jeter for five games last week. He analyzed Jeter in the dugout and the clubhouse and watched how he interacted with teammates on a club that has two shortstops with big league experience.

The manager liked what he observed. "Those are things I want to see," he said, lauding Jeter's quickness and fearlessness. "Those are things you can't get in a report."

Stump Merrill has managed Jeter for 25 games at Columbus, where the 6-foot-3-inch, 180-pounder, who wiggles his bat and has the hip-hop swagger of the basketball player he used to be, has batted .314 with 2 homers, 13 runs batted in, 7 steals and 5 errors.

When asked what has most impressed him, Merrill said, "Everything."

When asked what he needs to improve upon, Jeter replied, "Everything."

Although he declined to handicap Jeter's chances of reaching the Yankees next season, General Manager Gene Michael, a former shortstop, said: "He's the real thing. I liked what I saw of him. He's getting there."

Jeter does not believe the hype or at least he does not let himself believe it. He hit .329 in 69 games at Class A Fort Lauderdale, then was bumped to Class AA Albany, where he hit .377 in 34 games.

And Jeter is blossoming just when two Yankee shortstops — Mike Gallego and Randy Velarde—can become free agents.

"I don't know what's going to happen," said Jeter. "They're going to do what they want to do. But I always knew the Yankees don't move people too quickly, so I was a little surprised when I came here."

And Jeter will not help anyone figure it out. He is polite and hesitant to say anything inflammatory, and his upbringing is right out of a Showalter playbook. Jeter's father, Charles, a drug and alcohol counselor, and his mother, an accountant, have lectured him about not being self-centered and they gave him daily advice when reporters trekked to Columbus last week and focused on him.

"We want to make sure if he's talking to reporters that he's minding his P's and Q's," said Mrs. Jeter.

"He might fit right into our clubhouse," said Showalter.

Open the clubhouse door. Here is a sampling of Jeter's remarks:

"I don't like hearing people who only talk about themselves."

"I think defense should always come first."

"I try not to pay attention to the newspapers."

Obviously, Jeter will be judged on his play, not his plays on words, and his glove will determine whether he is Showalter's shortstop in 1995. If Showalter is comfortable with Jeter's defense, where his shortcomings have been a tendency to throw every ball to first at warp speed and to botch the routine play, he could appear in the Bronx. Just as Uncle Joe speculated. ●

Jeter stretches before his first major league game on May 29, 1995, at Seattle's Kingdome. (AP Photo/Gary Stewart)

"I'm still dreaming," Jeter said yesterday. "The way New York has embraced us after the championship, I can't put it into words. This is still a dream. I hope we can do it a few more years."

It's No Contest as Jeter Captures Rookie of the Year

By JACK CURRY • Published: November 5, 1996

Derek Jeter was supposed to be the question mark on the Yankees this season, even according to Manager Joe Torre. Could the rookie handle playing shortstop? Could he succeed in New York? What would happen to the Yankees if the youngster floundered?

Imagine how ludicrous those concerns seem now.

Jeter's stylish play forced those questions to vanish faster than World Series tickets. The only question Jeter had to answer yesterday was where he planned to display his newest trophy, the American League rookie of the year award he won in a landslide.

The 22-year-old Jeter garnered all 28 first-place votes in becoming the fifth American Leaguer since the award's inception 50 years ago to be a unanimous choice for the honor.

No one was surprised. Not even the normally humble Jeter.

After Jeter homered off Cleveland's Dennis Martinez and made a nifty over-the-shoulder catch in the Yankees' season opener, he immediately became a strong candidate for the award. When the glorious season progressed and Jeter became a special and instrumental part of the Yankees' magical ride, it became more obvious that he would be named the premier rookie.

"I'm still dreaming," Jeter said yesterday. "The way New York has embraced us after the championship, I can't put it into words. This is still a dream. I hope we can do it a few more years."

Jeter was the first Yankee to win the award since Dave Righetti in 1981, the second-youngest Yankee to be voted the award after Tony Kubek (21 years old in 1957) and the eighth Yankee over all. He easily outdistanced the Chicago White Sox right-hander James Baldwin.

California's Tim Salmon was the last rookie to win unanimously in the American League, in 1993.

"Unanimous?" joked Jeter. "I must have had some of my family voting in it."

Not really. With 5 points for a first-place

In an October 1996 game, Jeter, chasing a foul ball, collides with a fan who fell out of the seats. (G. Paul Burnett/The New York Times)

It's No Contest as Jeter Captures Rookie of the Yea[r]

ROWN

e Times

'Neal

n Way

itle?

lle O'Neal comes to Man-
eras, celebrities and ex-
llow. So tonight's Knicks-
game at Madison Square
or event, even though the
Association season is less
re is no doubt that Shaq
ower. But when his career
emembered more for his
hampionships?
World for Hollywood dur-
Neal joined one of the
l franchises. Magic John-
five titles during the
y of Laker centers is the
, featuring Kareem Abdul-
rlain and George Mikan,
Minneapolis Lakers before
west.
sign O'Neal to a $120 mil-
k backboards, make mov-
After four years in Orlan-
with a hole in his résumé:
nd unless he fills that void,
akers will pale in compari-
rs who preceded him.

where winning a champi-
of priorities. Those close
burning desire for a ring,
several.
disturbing facts. His re-
ocking totals have de-
he last three seasons. He
he art of free-throw shoot-
layer most likely to be
tuations.

Perhaps most
important, O'Neal
chose to leave a
franchise that was
a contender and
had Penny
Hardaway, a bril-
liant, young point
guard who may be
the best player
O'Neal will ever
play with. The Lak-
ers have a load of
talent but when
O'Neal left the
Eastern Confer-
ence, one could al-
most hear the Chi-
cago Bulls, the Indi-
ana Pacers and the
Knicks saying,
"Thank you, Shaq."
Certainly, O'Neal
has carved out a
sizable place in the
game for himself in
a short period of
time. Last week, the
eague's list of its 50 all-
. Wonder how guys like
ice Cheeks felt seeing
t list instead of their own?
he league's most excit-
players? Probably. But if
e on that list, a case could
ay as well.
layer? Without question.
ty make him impossible
one on one. He plays the
air. He is an entertainer,
s such as Nick Van Exel
eballos and Kobe Bryant
l.
e Garden the place to be
neet the Lakers in the fin-
ly face O'Neal twice this
his only visit to New
e drawbacks of expan-
watch Patrick Ewing
n, and while there is a ri-
hey have never met in
hey are no longer Atlan-

The Yankee Who Never Stopped Short

Yankees shortstop Derek Jeter
was unanimously selected the
American League rookie of the
year by the Baseball Writers
Association of America. He
joins some exclusive A.L.
rookie company.

UNANIMOUS WINNERS

1972	Carlton Fisk, Bos., C
1987	Mark McGwire, Oak., 1B
1990	Sandy Alomar Jr., Clev., C
1993	Tim Salmon, Cal., OF
1996	Derek Jeter, Yankees, SS

YANKEE WINNERS

1951	Gil McDougald, 3B
1954	Bob Grim, P
1957	Tony Kubek, OF
1962	Tom Tresh, SS-OF
1968	Stan Bahnsen, P
1970	Thurman Munson, C
1981	Dave Righetti, P
1996	Derek Jeter, SS

SHORTSTOP WINNERS

1953	Harvey Kuenn, Det.
1956	Luis Aparicio, Chi.
1960	Ron Hansen, Balt.
1962	Tom Tresh, Yankees
1979	Alfredo Griffin, Tor.
1982	Cal Ripken Jr., Balt.
1985	Ozzie Guillen, Chi.
1988	Walt Weiss, Oak.
1992	Pat Listach, Mil.
1996	Derek Jeter, Yankees

G. Paul Burnett/The New York Times
Derek Jeter at Yankee Stadium yesterday after being named A.L. rookie of the year.

Yank Shortsto Is Fifth to Win In Vote Sweep

By JACK CURRY

Derek Jeter was supposed to
question mark on the Yankees this
even according to Manager Joe
Could the rookie handle playing
stop? Could he succeed in New
What would happen to the Yankee
youngster floundered?
Imagine how ludicrous those co
seem now.
Jeter's stylish play forced thos
tions to vanish faster than World
tickets. The only question Jeter
answer yesterday was where he
to display his newest trophy, the
can League rookie of the year a
won in a landslide.
The 22-year-old Jeter garnered
first-place votes in becoming th
American Leaguer since the awa
ception 50 years ago to be a una
choice for the honor.
No one was surprised. Not ev
normally humble Jeter.
After Jeter homered off Clev
Dennis Martinez and made a nift
the-shoulder catch in the Yankees'
opener, he immediately became a
candidate for the award. When th
ous season progressed and Jeter
a special and instrumental part
Yankees' magical ride, it becam
obvious that he would be named
mier rookie.
"I'm still dreaming," Jeter said
day. "The way New York has em
us after the championship, I can'
into words. This is still a dream. I
can do it a few more years."
Jeter was the first Yankee to
award since Dave Righetti in 19
second-youngest Yankee to be vc
award after Tony Kubek (21 year
1957) and the eighth Yankee over
easily outdistanced the Chicago W
right-hander James Baldwin.
California's Tim Salmon was
rookie to win unanimously in the
can League, in 1993.
"Unanimous?" joked Jeter. "
have had some of my family votin
Not really. With 5 points for a fir
vote, 3 for second and 1 for thir
voting by two news media membe
each American League city, Je
cured 140 points. Baldwin not
points on 19 seconds and 7 thirds, D
Tony Clark had 30 and Baltimore'
Coppinger and Kansas City's Jose
tied for fourth with 6 points.
It was another wondrous day fo
who hugged his father, Charles, c
news conference at Yankee Stadi
thanked "Mr. Steinbrenner" an
Torre" for having patience wi
Jeter even suggested that the Y
could have demoted him to the
leagues after he had an uneventful
but that was never a consideration
Yankees wanted him to learn on

Continued on Page B14, Colum

A CURVEBALL FROM OWNERS

A plan is afoot to make the player
the pending labor agreement. Pa

O'Neal vs. Ewing, Now for One Night Only

By SELENA ROBERTS

PURCHASE, N.Y., Nov. 4 — Their
matchups have seemed more like pillow
fights, two egos bumping up against each
other until one would occasionally burst.
Words would fly like stuffing, but nothing
ever seemed to scar either Shaquille
O'Neal or Patrick Ewing.
They would go at it in the not-so-old
days, banging and crashing around in the
post, trading snarls and baskets. But in
four seasons, it never got overly nasty.
Maybe once or twice — like the "I'm the
man" bit — but it's not as if the two ever
loathed each other as much as some wanted them to.
"He shows me respect," Ewing said
today after practice. "We talked a little

bit at the All-Star Game. He's a great
player. What do you want me to say?"
How about saying that O'Neal has gone
Hollywood for taking $120 million to leave
Orlando for Los Angeles? How about
that?
"He probably made the best decision
for himself," Ewing said diplomatically.
But with his departure, O'Neal effec-
tively took what was at the least an eye-
catching, made-for-TV divisional mat-
chup and shrank it to a less significant
cameo appearance. That's what it will be
when O'Neal arrives with the Lakers on
Tuesday for the only Shaq sighting at
Madison Square Garden this season.
It won't be the same. There was always
something more to it when the young,

snotty-nosed Magic would rile veterans
like Ewing for infringing on the Knicks
establishment; when O'Neal's popularity
— like the overtaking of Ewing in All-Star
voting — would sting. Once, Ewing decided enough was enough after a Knicks
victory, saying: "He thinks he's the man.
I don't feel like he's the man, yet."
That was three years ago. There is still
something to prove when they meet, but
there has been a lot of growing and mel-
lowing on both sides since then.
"I think he's a great player," Ewing
said. "I don't know if he thinks I'm a great
player."
He smiled as he said it, knowing he will

Continued on Page B12, Column 3

Controversial Play and Loss Leave Rangers Kicking Themselves

COOLEST

**Lightning
Rangers**

By JOE LAPOINTE

The Rangers' four-game undefeated streak
embarrassing fashion last night at Madison Squa

"It's tremendous," said Charles Jeter. "Derek is doing what he wants to do. I'm most proud of the way he carries himself beyond the baseball end. As a parent, I'm proud of the way he handled himself."

vote, 3 for second and 1 for third in the voting by two news media members from each American League city, Jeter secured 140 points. Baldwin notched 64 points on 19 seconds and 7 thirds, Detroit's Tony Clark had 30 and Baltimore's Rocky Coppinger and Kansas City's Jose Rosado tied for fourth with 6 points.

It was another wondrous day for Jeter, who hugged his father, Charles, during a news conference at Yankee Stadium and thanked "Mr. Steinbrenner" and "Mr. Torre" for having patience with him. Jeter even suggested that the Yankees could have demoted him to the minor leagues after he had an uneventful spring, but that was never a consideration. The Yankees wanted him to learn on the job and he did. Quickly and emphatically.

"We had a lot of guys who were valuable," said Torre. "I don't think we had one guy, player-wise, who was more valuable than him."

Torre said last February that he hoped Jeter would bat .250 and play dependable defense. The rookie exceeded those goals by hitting .314—the highest among the 10 shortstops voted rookies of the year—with 10 homers, 78 runs batted in, 104 runs scored and 22 errors in 157 games.

He evolved into perhaps the Yankees' premier player following the All-Star Game break, batting .350 with 6 homers and 40 r.b.i. to finish the regular season with a flourish, clinch the rookie award and secure a $10,000 contractual bonus.

"His hitting blew me out of the tub," said Torre, a former National League batting champion. "I never expected anything like that. I said something about him hitting .250. Someone told me he'd hit more than .250. I said fine."

Though the rookie voting is completed when the regular season ends, Jeter was even more impressive in the pressure-packed October as veterans like Wade Boggs, Paul O'Neill and Tino Martinez struggled for the Yankees. Jeter had a .361 average in the postseason—including one unforgettable homer against Baltimore that was helped by an overzealous 12-year-old—with 3 r.b.i. and 12 runs scored. Jeter combined with Bernie Williams as twin Mr. Octobers and helped usher the Yankees to their first World Series title since 1978, never looking like a player who would be a college senior right now.

"It's tremendous," said Charles Jeter. "Derek is doing what he wants to do. I'm most proud of the way he carries himself beyond the baseball end. As a parent, I'm proud of the way he handled himself."

When Jeter was asked what would inspire him in 1997 after a grandiose debut, he responded: "To come back. It was incredible. The parade. How the city took to us. I want to be back year after year. There's nothing else I'd rather do than win some more." ●

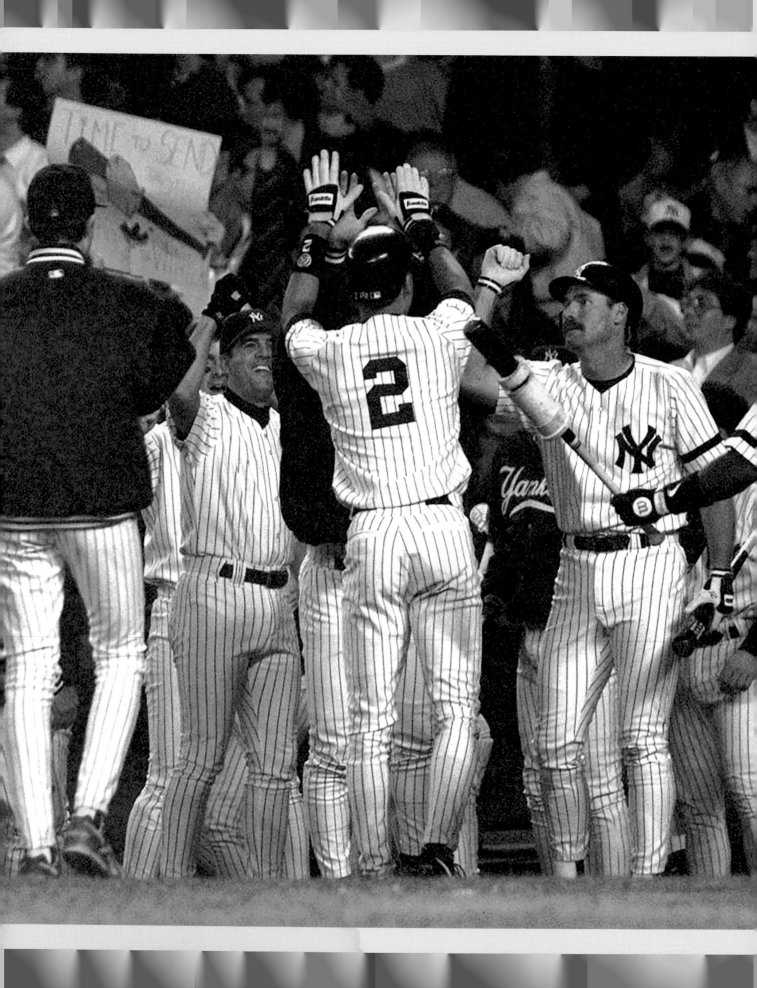

"Do I feel bad?" asked Jeter. "We won the game. Why should I feel bad? Ask them that."

Winning With a Boy's Help, Yankees Make No Apologies

By JACK CURRY • Published: October 10, 1996

One overzealous 12-year-old helped the Yankees rejoice on a day when all of their runs except Bernie Williams's game-winning homer were somewhat tainted. Still, after beating the Baltimore Orioles, 5-4, in 11 innings yesterday, the Yankees refused to apologize.

They won their first American League Championship Series game in 15 years, and did it with an assist from 12-year old Jeff Maier, a New Jersey boy with a keen eye and a quick glove. The young fan lived out every kid's dream, bringing his mitt to Yankee Stadium and getting a chance to use it. In the bottom of the eighth inning, Maier reached over the wall in right field to scoop a ball hit by New York's Derek Jeter away from Baltimore's right fielder and into the stands.

The Orioles screamed for interference, but it was ruled a home run. Although the umpire later second-guessed his call, the home run stood, the Yankees had tied the score at 4-4 and were on their way to a dramatic Game 1 victory.

Jeter wants to meet the boy to thank him and "Good Morning America" telephoned his house in Old Tappan, N.J., minutes after the game to try to schedule him on the show. The Orioles, who were rightfully perturbed, saw the incident as another indignity at the hands of a team that has now beaten them 11 out of 14 times this year.

Who could blame the Orioles? Leading off the bottom of the 11th, Williams rocked Randy Myers's 1-1 slider deep into the left-field seats. It was his fourth home run this October, and it vaulted the Yankees to their fourth straight come-from-behind triumph in the postseason. The Yankees were delirious, and Jeff Maier was delighted.

"It's unbelievable," Jeff said. "It's pretty cool."

Darryl Strawberry soaked in the evening's strange events, the start of what is expected to be a riveting series, and mused, "They'll be talking about this one for a long time."

"Do I feel bad?" asked Jeter. "We won the game. Why should I feel bad? Ask them that." ●

Jeter is congratulated after hitting a controversial fan-aided home run against the Orioles. (G. Paul Burnett /The New York Times)

"This is as good as any team I've ever had," Steinbrenner said, his hair slick from Champagne. "This is as good as any team that's ever played the game."

Yanks Sweep Series and Assure Legacy

By BUSTER OLNEY • Published: October 22, 1998

SAN DIEGO, Oct. 21— The Yankees have been a team greater than the sum of its parts all year, and when they secured their own corridor in history tonight, it was appropriate that a pitcher who had struggled in recent weeks pushed them over the finish line.

Andy Pettitte, dropped to the back of the Yankees' rotation for the World Series, applied the final piece to their mosaic tonight, pitching seven and a third shutout innings and outdueling Kevin Brown in a 3-0 victory over the San Diego Padres in Game 4. In achieving their first Series sweep since 1950 and seventh in their history, the Yankees wrapped up their 24th championship and the second in the last three years.

The Yankees set an American League record with 114 victories in the regular season, then eliminated Texas, three games to none, Cleveland, 4-2, and San Diego, 4-0. The Yankees finished the year with 125 victories and 50 losses in the regular season and postseason combined, shattering the previous record of 118. Their winning percentage of .714 is the third best in history for World Series winners, behind the 1927 Yankees (.722) and the 1909 Pittsburgh Pirates (.717). ●

Later, Jeter's shirt and face were wet from Champagne, a bottle in one hand and a cigar in the other. "I'm a little young to know about the teams back in the early 1900's," said the 24-year-old Jeter, "but we were 125 and 50, and there's not too many teams that can say that."

Jubilant Yankees swamp Mariano Rivera after finishing off the Padres to win the 1998 World Series. (Chang W. Lee/The New York Times)

"He used to joke that Derek was going to make more money in one year than he made in a lifetime," said Msgr. Thomas Madden, the pastor at Queen of Peace.

Grandfather Led Jeter To Value Hard Work

By JACK CURRY • Published: February 24, 1999

He took care of the same church, high school and elementary school for 36 years, fixing the electrical wiring, repairing faulty pipes and vacuuming the rugs around the altar. He was a blue-collar worker, never taking a day off. He rarely sneaked away to see Derek Jeter, his grandson, play for the Yankees in person. Not when he had to wake up at 4:30 A.M. the next day.

His name was William Connors, though everyone knew him as Sonny, and he was as much of a fixture at Queen of Peace Church in North Arlington, N.J., as the pews. If priests needed light bulbs for the sacristy, they called Sonny. If nuns needed someone to paint their living room, they called Sonny. He worked diligently as the head of maintenance, a routine that his grandson observed as a boy and emulated as a man.

"He never missed work, if he was sick or he had a bad day," Jeter said. "He always seemed to go and work every day. I think that's something I learned from him."

In answering questions about his dream life as the shortstop who will make $5 million this season for a team that has snatched two World Series championships in the last three years, Jeter admitted that he has distressing days, too. One of them occurred on New Year's Day when Sonny Connors died of a heart attack at 68. Many lose elderly relatives, but Jeter's memories vividly showed that even someone with a charmed existence has awful days.

"He touched a lot of people's lives," Jeter said. "He wasn't making millions of dollars, but he had just as much of an effect on someone's life as any one of us in here."

More than 800 people attended Connors's funeral, and the high school and elementary school were both closed as a tribute to him. The people who flocked to the funeral were the same people who had relied on Sonny to give their car a jump start, who sat near him at Mass after he opened the church at 6:30, who knew him from St. Michael's Church in Jersey City, where he also handled maintenance for more than 14 years, and who saved articles for him about his famous grandson.

"He used to joke that Derek was going to make more money in one year than he made

Jeter executing his famous jump throw. (Barton Silverman/The New York Times)

in a lifetime," said Msgr. Thomas Madden, the pastor at Queen of Peace. "He said he should have spent more time playing ball as a kid. But he was so proud of Derek. The only thing he used to pray for was that Derek wouldn't get hurt."

Jeter, who was a pallbearer at the funeral, gazed at the hundreds of mourners and realized that his special grandfather was special to a legion of admirers.

"People say you know who your friends were at your funeral," Jeter said. "Have you ever heard that expression? A lot of people showed up. A lot of people showed they cared, and a lot of people showed that he affected their lives in some way."

When Jeter was 10, his grandfather took him to work and showed him how to mow the football field. Jeter recalled that the grass was almost a foot high and he had a mower with a bag, so he had to stop dozens of times and empty it. Once Jeter finished the job hours later, Connors told him to start over because the grass had grown back.

"I never worked with him again," said Jeter, a smile creasing his face.

Sharlee Jeter, Derek's younger sister, referred to her grandfather's work ethic in a eulogy, saying: "He was a very strict boss. That's why Derek has no problems playing for George Steinbrenner."

Everyone inside the church laughed at the remark. It was another tribute to a man who spent half a century tending to two churches, a man who was a loving father to 14 and a man who taught his baseball-playing grandson about the pleasures of working hard.

"He was a wonderful person," the monsignor said. "It will be a long time before we see the likes of Sonny again. I've seen the way Derek carries himself, and in the long run, hopefully, he'll be the man his grandfather was. If he is, he'll really be accomplishing something in his life." ●

"He always seemed to go and work every day," Jeter said. "I think that's something I learned from him." (Richard Perry/The New York Times)

Charles Jeter is black and from Alabama and Dorothy Jeter is white and from New Jersey, and Derek seemed at ease with kids from all kinds of backgrounds.

Derek Jeter: The Pride of Kalamazoo

By BUSTER OLNEY • Published: April 4, 1999

Ask around Kalamazoo, and everybody seems to have only good things to say about Derek Jeter and his family. Derek was the type of kid, Evelyn Lal said, "that you wanted your kid to be friends with."

Shanti Lal, her son, befriended Derek in the fourth grade, in Mrs. Garzelloni's class at St. Augustine Cathedral School in Kalamazoo. "Derek was one of those kids you just never forget, and I would say that even if he wasn't playing baseball," said Shirley Garzelloni, who retired last year. "He was the kind of student any teacher would want to have. I was just struck with how much he cared about his fellow classmates."

He appeared a little shy and quiet, she thought, but had a composed confidence, even as a boy. He got along with everybody and succeeded without needing to be prodded or praised. "He was completely self-motivated, creative, never wasted any time," Garzelloni recalled. "There are kids who will say to you, 'I don't have anything to do'—not with Derek.

He always found something to do. I remember doing a report card and thinking, 'Does he realize just how intelligent he is?'"

As smart as he was, Garzelloni said, Jeter never carried himself as if he were any different from his classmates. Evelyn Lal said, "He's quiet, but at the same time, he's very smart—he knows how to fit in, to get along."

He was comfortable around different types of people and, his father suggested, that made sense. Charles Jeter is black and from Alabama and Dorothy Jeter is white and from New Jersey, and Derek seemed at ease with kids from all kinds of backgrounds.

There were the trials of youth: Charles Jeter remembered that once when Derek was perhaps 10 or 11, a teacher told them that Derek had said something cruel to a classmate. His parents chastised Derek, told him this was unacceptable. You treat people the way you want to be treated, they said, and Derek thought about this quietly, absorbing and learning.

"He was pretty much head and shoulders

Jeter hits the dirt against the Marlins in the 2003 World Series. (G. Paul Burnett/The New York Times)

But baseball was significant to him. His favorite team, Derek told his fourth-grade teacher, was the New York Yankees, and he wrote an essay in the eighth grade of his desire to play shortstop for the Yankees.

above his contemporaries, but he never came across as being arrogant," said Chris Oosterbaan—Jeter stills calls her "Mrs. O"—who taught writing and history to Jeter at St. Augustine when he was in the seventh and eighth grade. "He didn't paint a glowing picture of himself, and he didn't have this 'I'm really cool' attitude. He was very genuine and humble."

Jeter worked as a tutor in a computer laboratory in his last two years of high school at Kalamazoo Central, and Sally Padley, who taught Jeter in British literature, thought he conducted himself perfectly. "He just had an easy manner, no signs of conceit, and when he was helping people, he didn't make any of them feel less important," Padley said.

She taught him in the last hour of school, a time when some student-athletes departed to prepare for games. "He absolutely never asked for any special consideration," Padley recalled. "He never asked out of class, never bragged about his baseball."

But baseball was significant to him. His favorite team, Derek told his fourth-grade teacher, was the New York Yankees, and he wrote an essay in the eighth grade of his desire to play shortstop for the Yankees. Padley asked her 11th-grade students to create a coat of arms, unique to each of them and their personalities. In the center of Jeter's rendering, he included a picture of a Yankee at bat.

Dorothy and Charles Jeter were always involved, Derek's former teachers say, always at the teacher-parent conferences, supportive of their suggestions, interested in their input. Derek Jeter called his 11th-grade teacher "Mrs. Padley," and so, too, did his parents.

"They have extremely strong values," Padley said. "They are some of the best parents I've ever seen."

Charles Jeter was raised in a single-parent home, with a mother who encouraged him and expected him to be accountable for the way he treated others; Dorothy Jeter's parents supported her endeavors, as well, and together, the Jeters believed in encouraging their two children. When Derek said he wanted to be the shortstop for the Yankees, they told him that with hard work, anything was possible, and sometimes the four of them would go in their backyard to practice—Charles hitting ground balls, Derek fielding and throwing the ball to his younger sister, Sharlee, perhaps Dorothy pitching Wiffleball.

At the beginning of each school year, Charles and Dorothy Jeter sat down with a yellow legal pad and drew up a contract with Derek. They agreed to terms on grades, on sports, on extracurricular activities, on how to handle drugs, and the parents and their son would sign together.

Padley, Oosterbaan and Garzelloni all spoke of their belief that no matter how big a celebrity Jeter became, no matter how much money he made, he would be rooted. "Derek has a lot of things he's going to learn about people, and being in the eye of the public," Padley said. "But I believe he's going to remain a very

decent human being."

Jeter could never change—never let the success go to his head—and get away with it, he said recently. "I couldn't go home; I'm no different than anybody else," Jeter said, except that he has a pretty good job.

He's still Derek from Kalamazoo, with the same friends from high school, friends who are scattered around the country now. Doug Biro, a friend from the fourth grade, stopped by the other day to have dinner with him in Tampa, Fla.

Shanti Lal, his friend from Mrs. Garzelloni's class, visited him in the minor leagues in Columbus, Ohio, and in spring training two years ago. They grew up together, laughed together; Derek and Shanti and another friend had entered a talent contest, the three of them, as the Jackson Five, with wigs and blue suits.

Lal planned to go to medical school, but on May 4, 1997, his sport utility vehicle rolled over on Interstate 94, and he was thrown from it and killed. Dorothy Jeter was the first to arrive at Evelyn Lal's house. Derek heard the news, and later, past midnight, he called home and spoke to his father. "I can't believe it," he said. "Shanti's gone."

In the midst of a baseball season, Jeter could not attend his friend's service, but he wrote a letter, and his sister read the words aloud, about his friendship with Shanti, how long they had known each other, all their shared experiences, their last days in Tampa together.

"Derek, he's a very good kid," Evelyn Lal said last week. "He is the type of kid I want my kids to be with, my Shanti." ●

Jeter ducks a high inside pitch against the Texas Rangers, Sept. 30, 1998. (Ozier Muhammad/The New York Times)

"The Yankees were awesome," said John Smoltz, the losing pitcher. "They played absolutely perfect. I can't think of one mistake they made."

Crucial Errors of Omission Also Haunt the Braves

By MURRAY CHASS • Published: October 28, 1999

The box score of their final game of 1999 will show that the Atlanta Braves committed no errors. The box score, however, doesn't always tell the whole story. Ryan Klesko, the Braves' first baseman, failed to make a makeable play in the third inning of Game 4 last night, and the Yankees, as they did during the entire post-season, capitalized on it for a 4-1 victory and two record-tying World Series feats.

The victory, generated by the two-run single Tino Martinez was credited with on his hard grounder to Klesko, was the Yankees' 12th in a row in the World Series over a four-year span and gave the Yankees two successive World Series sweeps, only the third time that feat has been achieved. Both of these records, 12 consecutive victories and sweeps in successive seasons, were set by—who else?—the Yankees of earlier eras.

As diluted as major league baseball may be because of repeated expansion, the Yankees have nevertheless established one of the great runs of all time. They have won three World Series championships in the past four years, making them the first team since the Oakland Athletics of 1972-73-74 to win that many times in such a short period.

"The Yankees were awesome," said John Smoltz, the losing pitcher. "They played absolutely perfect. I can't think of one mistake they made." ●

Jeter runs back to the clubhouse after sweeping the Atlanta Braves in the 1999 World Series. (AP Photo/Mark Lennihan)

Not once did anyone raise the question of whether Jeter was worth a staggering salary, or if the quality of his play would erode once he had banked Steinbrenner's millions.

Jeter Offers Leadership Along With His Talent

By BUSTER OLNEY • Published: January 20, 2000

Yankees officials congregate in Tampa, Fla., every fall to discuss their players. They meet in a room that has walls painted in Yankee Stadium blue and adorned with framed pictures of Yankee greats. The table is rectangular, and George Steinbrenner, the principal owner, sits at the head.

Derek Jeter's name was raised last November, when Steinbrenner and his platoon of advisers knew that they would soon need to commit tens of millions of dollars to keep the shortstop under contract. But not once did anyone raise the question of whether Jeter was worth a staggering salary, or if the quality of his play would erode once he had banked Steinbrenner's millions.

And as soon as the negotiations on Jeter's seven-year, $118.5 million deal are concluded—and depending on how the contract is structured, the final total may slightly increase—he will easily slide back into his place in the Yankees' clubhouse, where he is respected and not resented for all that he has.

Jeter was in Tampa yesterday, making his usual appearance at the Yankees' minor league complex for a workout. Steinbrenner was not returning phone calls and was said to be miffed that word of the contract got out before being completed. Others in the organization speculated yesterday that the sometimes-stubborn owner might delay the announcement of the agreement so that he could regain a bit of control.

But the deal cannot be put off indefinitely, with spring training less than a month away. Jeter and Steinbrenner live in the same area and could wrap up the negotiations at any time, although Jeter has commitments that will take him outside of Florida over the next week.

His teammates will inevitably tease him about his new contract when spring training begins, and then the matter will fade amid the relentless exhibition schedule. Jeter is thick with confidence, but from the time he was a rookie, he has deferred to teammates like Paul O'Neill

A BERKOW
orts of The Times

oss's Views re Merely ocus Focus

EORGE STEINBRENNER, who is to
baseball what Matthew Brady, Edward
Steichen and Richard Avedon are to
ography, is an expert on focus.

is is what the Yankees' principal owner
Monday in regard to the Mets' charge af-
eir weekend series that Roger Clemens
osely hit Mike Piazza in the head with a 92-
an-hour fastball, and, to a markedly lesser
ee, the protested interference call against
irst baseman Todd Zeile.

hey had to take the focus off the fact that
got their fannies handed to them this
," Steinbrenner said. "I'm not sure it was-
very wise public relations move for them
ke the focus off the way they were beaten.
think Bobby Valentine and his people
d love to take the focus off that, and have
eople forget about the results."

at Steinbrenner — we can just picture
under a black cloth and behind that old
camera — is really doing is seeking to re-
the focus to where he believes the focus
uddenly become unfocused. That is, on his
x Bombers. But his defense of his pitcher,
e understandable, is tasteless, if not repre-
ible.

s undeniable, of course, that the Yankees
the Mets three out of four games last
end, and four out of six in the Subway Se-
his year. And forget for a moment that an
sing player could very well have been
, or severely maimed for life by a pitcher
e salary Steinbrenner pays, but recall his
rtise on focus. Examples are long, and leg-
ry:

Barton Silverman
ge Steinbrenner

"I didn't fire the
man": Steinbren-
ner, at a news con-
ference announcing
the departure of his
manager Dick
Howser in 1980.
Then in 1987: "Fir-
ing Dick Howser
and not re-signing
Reggie Jackson
were the two big-
gest mistakes I
ever made with the
Yankees." And
there was his de-
fense of himself
with his fists in 1981
when attacked by
an elevator in Los
Angeles after the
Yanks were beaten
in the World Series
by the Dodgers.
And every time the
Yanks make a stu-
pid trade: "It was
my baseball peo-

And whenever they make a successful
e — well, you get the picture.

w, Steinbrenner may bridle at these ob-
ations, saying that that stuff is old hat, but
we are with a new hat that looks very
n like the old fedora.

einbrenner may very well be a flyspeck
ide of objective in his viewpoint. And it
here that the umpire's call, which award-
uck Knoblauch second base after initially
g thrown out when he was forced to run
d Zeile, was the correct one. Either Zeile,
mily spectating directly in the base path,
anny and knew better, or he's a dolt and
. Either way, the Mets' protest of the
e to the league office should be dismissed.
e Clemens pitch, which produced a con-
on in Piazza despite his wearing a plastic
et for protection, is another matter. It's a
worn axiom, as Steinbrenner adds, that
all pitchers "have to live on the inside."
brushbacks are a century-old part of base-
But that doesn't make it right. Steinbren-
aid: "I know Roger, I know he's a family
who loves his kids, and there's no way a fu-

Jeter Gives the Fans an All-Star Performance

Associated Press

Derek Jeter, who went 3 for 3, stroking a double in the first inning. He drove in two runs with a single in the fourth inning.

Associated Press

It was a night for families and smiles at the All-Star
Game. Players brought out their children before the
introductions, and Chipper Jones, right, was congratulated by Sammy Sosa after a third-inning home run.

Reuters

Helps Them Forget The Injured Missing

By JACK CURRY

ATLANTA, July 11 — Derek Jeter
tucked his jersey into his uniform pants
and listed the people who were at the All-
Star Game to watch him start for the
American League tonight. Jeter mentioned his parents, his sister and three of
his friends from
New York, shaking   **AMERICAN   6**
his head as he   **NATIONAL   3**
talked about secur-
ing enough decent tickets. But Jeter
should not have stopped his list at six
people.

Besides Jeter's family and friends,
there were 51,317 other fans who were at
Turner Field to watch him, too. It happened that way because a game that was
missing marquee players like Mark
McGwire, Ken Griffey Jr., Alex Rodriguez
and Pedro Martínez, and was being called
the All-Scar Game, developed into another
enticing stage for the amazing Jeter.

Jeter stroked three hits, knocked in two
runs and scored one run to power the
American League past the National
League, 6-3, and become the first Yankee
to win the most valuable player award in
the All-Star Game. Manager Joe Torre
chose his shortstop as the starter after
Rodriguez sustained a concussion last
Friday, and Jeter poked a two-run single
off the Mets' Al Leiter in the fourth inning
to break a 1-1 tie in helping the A.L. win
the game for the fourth straight year.

"You have to play a lot of years before
you can be considered a Yankee great,
and I've only played four years," Jeter
said. "This is my fifth year. Hopefully, I
can play a few more years and start that
debate."

The debate has already started. Yogi
Berra, Mickey Mantle, Roger Maris, Reg-
gie Jackson, Thurman Munson, Dave Win-
field, Reggie Jackson, Don Mattingly,
Rickey Henderson, Paul O'Neill and Mari-
ano Rivera have all played in All-Star
Games as Yankees since the M.V.P. was
first given in 1962, but none ever won what
Jeter did tonight. The National Baseball
Hall of Fame took Jeter's black Louisville
Slugger P72 bat that he used for all three
hits back to Cooperstown, N.Y.

"Right now, I'm very happy, obviously," Jeter said. "But I think in due time,
when I sit down and get a chance to reflect
on it, then you realize how special it is.
And I wasn't aware that no other Yankee
had won this award, and it's kind of hard
to believe."

The fans lined up outside Turner Field
early on a steamy day. Some had their
tickets, some were searching for tickets,
and most were eager to watch the finest
players in baseball. Well, they were eager
to see most of the best players in baseball.
The list of injured players was stunning
for its size and stature.

Players like McGwire, Griffey, Rodriguez, Martínez, Cal Ripken Jr., Mike Piazza, Barry Bonds and Greg Maddux are not
once-in-a-lifetime All-Stars. They are future Hall of Famers and the type of players fans thirst to watch. But all eight, plus

Continued on Page D3

Hoping to Face the Champ Again

Americans Aren't Known as Fencers. Cliff Bayer Says Otherwise.

By RICHARD SANDOMIR

Cliff Bayer's fencing coach rarely let him forget the
exquisite timing and savvy ruses that make Sergei Goloubitski the world's premier foilist and an Olympic gold
medal favorite. Yefim Litvan's praise of Goloubitski, a
fellow Ukrainian, sounded to Bayer more like taunting

Edmonton Pipeline Delivers Low

By JASON DIAMOS

The migration from Edmonton to New
York continues. Ron Low, a former Oiler
player and coach, will be appointed the

It was remarkable, some teammates felt, that someone that young could naturally take charge in that situation. But Jeter is leading the Yankees into this century now.

and David Cone and to Manager Joe Torre. And in their eyes, Jeter has ascended to a natural pre-eminence.

He is good-natured and well-liked, but there is an edge to Jeter, seen at those moments when his sense of right and wrong is offended—as it was with incidents with Chad Curtis and David Wells.

Curtis, traded to the Texas Rangers last month, has strong personal and religious beliefs and led the team's prayer group. He intermittently approached Jeter about joining the group, and Jeter put him off politely and directly, telling him he respected his beliefs but chose not to participate.

While an uneasy relationship might have resulted, the two coexisted easily—until last summer, when Curtis angrily chastised Jeter after a fight with Seattle for fraternizing with Jeter's good friend Alex Rodriguez during the brawl.

Curtis raised the issue first in the dugout and then in the clubhouse, in front of a crowd of reporters; thereafter, Jeter kept his feelings for Curtis beneath a thin veil of disgust. When asked about the incident weeks later, Jeter responded that nothing Curtis had said bothered him—dismissive words, wielded like a fly swatter. Curtis, after all, had made the mistake of forcing their differences into the newspapers, and Jeter would not back down.

It was interesting that after Curtis was traded, officials around baseball assumed—wrongly—that his confrontation with Jeter led directly to his exile, a sign that Jeter's stature and credibility were established after just four years in the majors.

In 1998, when Jeter was 24 and the Yankees would win 125 games, Torre was in the habit of resting his regulars in September. He removed two of his outfielders in the sixth inning of a game in Baltimore, and a blooper subsequently fell between Jeter and the subs, to the chagrin of Wells, the pitcher. The left-hander turned to the dugout in frustration and spread his hands, as if to say, "Are we trying?"

Jeter saw the uncharitable gesture and began yelling at Wells, telling him in so many words that no one on this team does that stuff. Wells, 11 years older, later backed down and apologized. It was remarkable, some teammates felt, that someone that young could naturally take charge in that situation. But Jeter is leading the Yankees into this century now, and will be well-compensated for his presence. ●

Derek Jeter, Mariano Rivera, and Jorge Posada celebrate after defeating the Seattle Mariners in the 2000 American League Championship Series. (Vincent Laforet/ The New York Times)

"This is by far the best team we've played," he said, meaning the Mets as a World Series opponent. "All the games could have gone either way."

Jeter, the M.V.P., Says This Title Is Most Gratifying

By DAVE ANDERSON • Published: October 27, 2000

With a home run in each of the last two games and a .409 batting average, Yankee shortstop Derek Jeter was named the most valuable player of the Subway Series last night, but he deferred the honor.

"You could've picked a name out of the hat; we have 25 M.V.P.'s," he said. "First game, Vizcaino. What O'Neill's done, our pitching staff, our bullpen, Luis Sojo. You don't rely on one guy."

His cap on backward, Jeter, 26, was wearing a gray World Series champions sweatshirt that was wet with Champagne spray, but he entered the interview area carrying a bottle of water.

"This is by far the best team we've played," he said, meaning the Mets as a World Series opponent. "All the games could've gone either way. Every year is a different story, but I'd be lying if I said this wasn't more gratifying. Oakland was the hottest team when we played 'em, Seattle was tough, and the Mets were the best team I've seen in five years."

In his five seasons, Jeter has earned four World Series rings, including one in each of the last three years.

For the Subway Series, he had 9 hits in 22 at-bats, including two doubles, a triple and two homers. His first-pitch homer off Bobby J. Jones set the tone for the Yankees' 3-2 victory in Game 4 and his one-out homer off Al Leiter created a 2-2 tie in the sixth inning of last night's 4-2 victory.

The homers supplied his two runs batted in for the Series and sparked his .864 slugging average. He also walked three times. Jeter's 19 total bases set a five-game Series record. He tied five-game records with his nine hits and six runs scored.

Asked if this Series victory was a last hurrah for this Yankee team's core group, he said: "No one is focused on next year. We're going to enjoy this before we start thinking about next year." And when he was asked what his reaction would be if Joe Torre were to retire as manager, he smiled.

"If he retires, I'm going to retire," Jeter said. "He continues to push the right buttons. He's got a magic wand. You can't say enough about him as a manager. He's a player's manager. He lets you play. He doesn't get on you unless you make mental mistakes. He has a lot of confidence in everybody." ●

SUBWAY SERIES

Take **7** to
Shea Stadium

With SportsThursday

The New York Times

THURSDAY, OCTOBER 26, 2000   L+   D1

4

Yanks Push Mets Toward the Edge

Jeter's First-Pitch Homer Sets the Tone for Yet Another One-Run Victory

Torre Acts As if Series Is on the Line

By HARVEY ARATON

It turned out that Joe Torre had even less faith in Denny Neagle with a lead last night than Bobby Cox did four years ago. Mike Piazza had hit one tape-measure foul ball against Neagle in the first inning. He'd belted a two-run homer into the Shea Stadium picnic area in the third.

Sports of The Times

By the fifth inning, with Neagle one out from being the pitcher of record on the winning side, Torre would not allow the Mets' Piazza to feast his eyes on Neagle again.

Out went a frowning Neagle. In came David Cone, resurrected, if only for one hitter before Torre pinch-hit Jose Canseco for him with two out and two on in the sixth. Torre, not playing around, pressing all buttons for a 3-2 Game 4 victory, was, in effect, admitting last night that the Yankees were playing with World Series fire.

He had seen this kind of spark in the bush before get out of control, become a blaze that burned down an Atlanta Braves World Series dynasty-in-the-making.

The last time Neagle started Game 4 of a World Series, in 1996, my wife turned off her night light after a few lopsided innings and suggested I do likewise. "Go to sleep," she grumbled. "This game's over."

She slept right through the Yankees' sixth-inning rally, when Neagle was lifted by Cox after giving back half his six-run lead, and then Jim Leyritz's three-run homer off Mark Wohlers as the Yankees rallied to even the Series.

It was a fateful blast, the moment that launched Torre's Yankees through the arch of greatness, to where they had already spent much of the 20th century. The Braves, defending champions, hardened tomahawk choppers, were a few measly outs from going there themselves. Neagle, who had not joined the Braves until August 1996, left Atlanta with only memories of postseason failure.

"Every year, at least when I was with Atlanta, we'd make base-running mistakes," he said. "Nobody would come up with a hit. When we needed to make that one big pitch, somebody else would get a hit against us. These guys in this clubhouse — with guys like El Duque, with Jeter, with Bernie, now Justice — it's a different guy every year. Somebody has to come through for you, and it always happens every year on this team."

Happened three of the last four years. Happened this fall, even after the Yankees' September slide, until their 14-game Series streak was halted in Game 3. But

Continued on Page D3

By BUSTER OLNEY

The Mets needed to build on the momentum of their Game 3 victory, but it didn't even last a single pitch in Game 4 of the Subway Series last night. Derek Jeter clubbed Bobby Jones's first offering of the game for a home run, giving the Yankees a lead they never relinquished, and now the Yankees are on the verge of another championship.

| YANKEES | 3 |
| METS | 2 |

Yankees lead series, 3-1

A relay team of Yankees' relievers — David Cone, Jeff Nelson, Mike Stanton and Mariano Rivera — maintained a 3-2 lead from the fifth inning through the ninth at Shea Stadium, giving the Yankees a three-games-to-one lead in the World Series. Jeter hit a home run and a triple and scored twice, and Paul O'Neill, who has been revitalized in this series, had a triple and single and made a sliding catch to start the bottom of the eighth inning.

Cone got one out in the fifth in relief of Denny Neagle, Nelson got four outs, Stanton two and Rivera came on to pitch the final two innings.

The Yankees staggered to the finish line at the end of the regular season, barely survived the first round of the playoffs, and are playing with the knowledge that some of the veterans who have been integral to the recent championships probably won't be in pinstripes next year. But now they are one victory away from becoming the first team since the Oakland Athletics of 1972-74 to win three consecutive championships, and the first team since the advent of free agency in 1976, a change that made it far more difficult for clubs to hold a core of players together.

Al Leiter will try to keep the Mets' hopes alive tonight in Game 5 at Shea Stadium,

Continued on Page D3

The Mets' starter, Bobby J. Jones, watching Derek Jeter's home run on the first pitch of Game 4 last night.

Mets Missing The Reliables, Old and New

By MURRAY CHASS

Not much time has elapsed since Timo Perez and Edgardo Alfonzo auditioned for their roles as the Mets' Dynamic Duo. In Game 4 of the National League Championship Series against St. Louis, Perez and Alfonzo, the first two batters in the lineup, drilled two of the five doubles the Mets hit in the first inning. In Game 5, they stroked successive singles in the first inning, propelling the Mets to a quick 3-0 lead.

On Baseball

In the World Series, however, Perez and Alfonzo have become the Mets' Dynamic Duds. Each is hitting .125 with 2 hits in 16

Jeter Shares the Success Of Sister's Winning Fight

By JACK CURRY • Published: May 13, 2001

Derek Jeter sat beside Joe Torre in the dugout during Friday night's game, as he had done hundreds of times before, and told his manager that it was a good day. Then Jeter told Torre exactly why it was a good day. Jeter's sister, Sharlee, no longer had to worry about having Hodgkin's disease. Torre was shocked because he did not even know the 21-year-old woman had had cancer.

"It knocked me back a little," Torre said.

Jeter found out last November that his little sister, the feisty one, the one he had always considered the best shortstop in the family, had Hodgkin's disease. It was a month after Jeter had been named the most valuable player of the World Series and two months before he signed a 10-year, $189 million contract. Those baseball issues were secondary to his sister's undergoing chemotherapy treatments every two weeks for six months.

When the chemo finished on Thursday and doctors told Sharlee she would not need radiation treatments because there were no more signs of cancer, the Jeters were relieved.

Other than telling a few friends, Jeter had kept his sister's condition private. The only reason he revealed the news, on Friday, was because "now it's a success story," he said.

The Yankees have been a remarkably successful team, but hardly immune to the human problems facing any other group of three dozen or so workers. Sharlee's situation is the latest example of how the Yankees' players and coaches and their families are just as susceptible to tragedy and sickness as their fans and their families. Torre and Mel Stottlemyre, the team's pitching coach, overcame cancer; Darryl Strawberry is fighting it a second time; Paul O'Neill, Scott Brosius and Luis Sojo buried their fathers while the Yankees won a title in 1999; Chuck Knoblauch's father has Alzheimer's disease; and Bernie Williams has missed 10 games and may miss more because his father has a terminal illness.

But Jeter? Just 26 years old, he has four World Series rings, owns the second-richest contract in sports history, has dated Mariah Carey and Miss Universe, has a foundation

Derek Jeter stands with his sister Sharlee, his mother Dorothy, and his father Dr. Charles Jeter, as Derek is honored for his 3,000th career hit. (AP Photo/Bill Kostroun)

"Our family is not immune to anything that goes on in society," Jeter said.

that helps steer children away from drugs and alcohol and has the job he wanted since he was 8 years old. Most fans see Jeter playing shortstop every day, or see him blast a game-winning three-run homer, as he did yesterday in an 8-5 victory over the Baltimore Orioles, and speculate about how splendid his life is. Cancer disrupts that portrait.

"Our family is not immune to anything that goes on in society," Jeter said. "We never expect nothing like this to hit our family. It's just one of those things you have to deal with and, fortunately, it's over with."

Jeter is so close to Sharlee that they sometimes speak five times a day, and that was before she became ill. Sharlee gave a speech about Derek when Kalamazoo Central High School in Michigan honored him in 1996, thanking her brother for his honesty and support and calling him her hero. Jeter cried as she spoke and has the speech framed over his desk at home in Tampa, Fla.

Even after homering yesterday, Jeter is batting .289 with 2 homers and 17 runs batted in and 7 errors, subpar statistics for him that are partly attributable to shoulder and quadriceps injuries that have nagged him since the spring. Jeter steadfastly refused to link his listless start to his sister's illness.

"It was more difficult for her," Jeter said. "We don't want to make it out that it was more difficult for me. She's the one that was going through it."

While Torre said that Dorothy Jeter, Derek's mother, had told Torre's wife, Ali, that Sharlee was sick, Ali Torre did not pry for specifics. There is no way to gauge how much Jeter was affected by seeing Sharlee lose some of her hair, but Torre, who had prostate cancer, said "the whole family is affected" by cancer.

"It's certainly part of him," Torre said. "He's not going to say that. There's a lot going on. That's what makes it tough to play. You still have all the problems other people have, but you can't call in sick here."

Sharlee Jeter was an excellent high school softball player, and her dream was to attend Michigan and play in the Olympics, but she changed her plans, in part, because she was constantly compared to Derek. "He didn't have that shadow over him," she once said. "I had it every day of my life."

After she fell in November, she felt lumps on her neck and was told by a nurse at Spelman College in Atlanta that she probably had a pulled muscle. When the lumps remained, she had tests and the Hodgkin's was found. Sharlee continued a reduced class schedule at Spelman while splitting her treatments between Atlanta and Manhattan.

Sharlee is disappointed that she will not graduate with her class this month and will have to wait until December to earn her bachelor's degree in mathematics, but Jeter told her to "look at the big picture." The big picture is that Sharlee strolled into Yankee Stadium on Friday night to watch her brother play for the Yankees and walked in cancer-free.

"She's 21 years old, man," Jeter said. "You don't expect this to happen at such a young age. But the good news is she doesn't have cancer anymore." ●

Jeter ices his sore right shoulder after a 2001 playoff game against Seattle. (Barton Silverman/The New York Times)

"It's a look that you don't teach. It's a look that you have, that fire in your belly, that love for competition."

Add Catch To Jeter's Catalog Of Heroics

By STEVE POPPER • Published: October 16, 2001

Derek Jeter is the latest in the line of Yankee luminaries, so it was a fitting, if odd, moment when the Hall of Famer Phil Rizzuto paid homage to him before Game 5 in the division series against Oakland last night at Yankee Stadium. Rizzuto, on the field to throw out the ceremonial first pitch, dismissed the windup and pitch and instead mimicked Jeter's sensational defensive play in Game 3, when he backhanded the ball to the plate. That play allowed catcher Jorge Posada to tag out Jeremy Giambi.

The task might be a bit tougher for the 83-year-old Rizzuto if he ever wants to emulate Jeter's latest highlight.

Last night in the eighth inning, Jeter displayed a toughness and determination that few would be able to duplicate. And it is safe to guess that fewer would even bother to try.

After he had already knocked in the go-ahead run four innings earlier, Jeter and the Yankees were trying to preserve their tenuous two-run advantage. Jason Giambi led off the inning with a single against Mariano Rivera, and Terrence Long came up as the tying run.

He lofted a foul pop toward the third-base line that veered into the stands. Jeter burst toward the wall, calling off Scott Brosius. He leaned into the stands as the ball plopped into his glove. Then Jeter flipped onto his back onto the cement surface.

Brosius took the ball from him and threw a bullet to second base, trying unsuccessfully to catch Eric Chavez, who was tagging up from first. Concrete could not slow Jeter any more than the A's could.

"Derek, from 1996 when I first met the young man, has that look in his eye," Yankees Manager Joe Torre said. "It's a look that you don't teach. It's a look that you have, that fire in your belly, that love for competition. This kid, with that play the other day thinks cool in hot situations. He never had regard for putting his body in peril, or looking bad with a bad swing. We have many of them, but he's a true leader at a very early age."

But if Jeter is setting new standards, he still takes his place humbly. He refers to Rizzuto as Mr. Rizzuto, and to his manager as Mr. Torre.

"The Flip" — one of the most famous plays in the recent baseball history — Jeter tosses the ball backhand to Jorge Posada to get Oakland's Jeremy Giambi at the plate in the 2001 postseason. (Chang W. Lee/The New York Times)

"You make your own breaks," Jeter said. "You have to worry about the things you can control, but I think you go out and make your own breaks."

And like his flip in Game 3, which displayed an uncanny penchant for being in the right place at the right time, last night's catch was just another play to Jeter.

"When you're playing in postseason, you have to take every out," Jeter said. "If there is an opportunity to have an out, especially with that team, a runner on base and anyone is capable of hitting it out of the park, you just try to make the catch."

The highlight reels are a thought for another day, especially for someone who has four World Series rings in his five major league seasons. Jeter ignored the historical implications of his defensive efforts as well as the first-inning single that tied Pete Rose for the career record for most postseason hits with 86, or the 87th hit that followed in the sixth inning when he doubled to move alone to the top of the list.

Last night, Jeter said he was concerned only with getting an out, getting a victory and moving on.

Asked if he realized how difficult the catch was or how difficult the Yankees entire task was, coming back from a two-game deficit to capture the three-of-five-game series, he replied: "No. I mean, probably when you get a chance to reflect on it when the season is over, then you realize how difficult it was. We're good at taking it one game at a time.

"We were down two games and we had Mussina on the mound. That was a huge game for us to get us back in the series. Once we won that game, I think everyone in here felt as though we were going to win."

It can feel that way when one wins as often as Jeter has. When questions raised the notion of momentum or breaks going the Yankees way, his game face drew as taut as it had on the field.

"You make your own breaks," Jeter said. "You have to worry about the things you can control, but I think you go out and make your own breaks."

Jeter then was ordered to report to the trainer's room to get iced. It was that sort of night, when he had to ignore the begging chant of the crowd for a curtain call after the catch because he was being inspected by the trainer.

And if Jeter could not appreciate the significance of his accomplishments, the defensive gems or the .444 batting average in the series, others did.

"I've never seen an athlete dominate any sport—football, basketball, or baseball—the way he did in this playoff series," George Steinbrenner, the Yankees' owner, said. ●

Jeter exults after hitting the game-winning home run in the bottom of 10th inning of Game 4 against the Arizona Diamondbacks in the 2001 World Series. (G. Paul Burnett/The New York Times)

"I'm a great believer in history, and I look at all the other leaders down through Yankee history, and Jeter is right there with them."

Steinbrenner Appoints Jeter Captain of the Yankees

By TYLER KEPNER • Published: June 4, 2003

Derek Jeter has been an established Yankees star for years, and the highest-paid player on George Steinbrenner's team since February 2001. But Steinbrenner, the principal owner, waited until today to make official what the players in the clubhouse already knew: that Jeter is the captain of the Yankees.

Steinbrenner did not show up for the announcement at Great American Ball Park before the Yankees lost to the Cincinnati Reds, 4-3, choosing instead to stay in Tampa, Fla., to oversee today's amateur draft. But it was Steinbrenner's decision alone, and he appointed Jeter at this moment—on the road, with the team still shaking off a slump—for a reason.

"I think he can hopefully pull them together," Steinbrenner said in a telephone interview today. "I think he can give them a little spark. I just feel it's the right time to do it. People may say, 'What a time to pick.' Well, why not? He represents all that is good about a leader. I'm a great believer in history, and I look at all the other leaders down through Yankee history, and Jeter is right there with them."

Jeter became the 11th captain—Babe Ruth, Lou Gehrig and Thurman Munson are among the others—and the first since Don Mattingly retired after the 1995 season. Steinbrenner discussed the appointment with Jeter last weekend in Detroit and again this morning. "He just says he wants me to be a leader, like I have been," Jeter said. "The impression I got is just continue to do the things I've been doing."

Steinbrenner was not ready to make the appointment over the winter, when a question about it prompted his famous rant about Jeter's supposed lack of focus. Jeter's measured response to the criticism made an impression on Steinbrenner, who thinks Jeter can help Manager Joe Torre as a leader.

"He's a young man that's handled it very well," Steinbrenner said. "He said what he thought. He's always available, ready to face the questions, win or lose. I think he can be a big help to Joe Torre. I think he and Joe will work great together."

Steinbrenner has been eager to fix something with the Yankees since their 3-12

Jeter and George Steinbrenner talking about the club at spring training. (Barton Silverman/The New York Times)

"When he needs to talk, people are going to listen," Posada said.

skid last month. He has expressed doubt about the effectiveness of Torre's coaching staff and has had almost no contact with Torre this season. He did not consult him on the Jeter decision.

Torre said he did not want to play down Jeter's honor but did not think Jeter could help him do his job better, as Steinbrenner had suggested.

"I don't see my job being any different, as far as helping," Torre said, "because I don't know what he could tell someone if they have a question to ask me. It can't be a negative, but I don't think players are going to listen to him more now that he's captain. He's always had that respect."

The day after the Yankees were swept by Texas two weeks ago, Jeter spoke at a team meeting in Boston. Jeter was injured during the Yankees' hot start, and according to catcher Jorge Posada, he challenged his teammates. "What I saw on TV is this, and when I got here, I don't see the same thing," Jeter said.

Jeter is able to get his message across in private conversations and group settings, said Posada, who has long considered him the captain. "When he needs to talk, people are going to listen," Posada said.

Steinbrenner clearly places great emphasis on the captaincy. He sent two of his general partners, his son Hal and his son-in-law Steve Swindal, for the announcement, as well as General Manager Brian Cashman, whose wife is due to deliver the couple's second child any day.

Posada was among those puzzled by the timing of the announcement. "Why Cincinnati?" he said. "Why not do it in New York?" Cashman was asked that at a news conference.

"This is something he's thought about for a period of time, and he made his decision," Cashman said, referring to Steinbrenner. "Is it something he was going to sit on and wait until we came home, or go forward with? The reality in that clubhouse is, informally, people recognized him as probably the captain anyway. Now the Boss has recognized him in a formal way, and that's a great honor."

It is also a great responsibility, one that could put Jeter, even without a C on his jersey, in Steinbrenner's sights when things go wrong.

Jeter dismissed that idea.

"I don't see how it would," Jeter told reporters. "I talk to you guys every day."

But dealing with the news media is just one aspect of Jeter's new role. Steinbrenner is putting his faith in Jeter, and that always carries significant demands. In the statement the team released, Steinbrenner used his favorite quotation from Gen. Douglas MacArthur: "There is no substitute for victory."

Cajoling his teammates to victory will clearly be a mandate for Jeter.

"You do what your gut tells you," Steinbrenner said. "My gut tells me this would be a good time for Derek Jeter to assume leadership. He is a great leader by the way he performs and plays. I told him I want him to be the type of cavalry officer who can sit in the saddle. You can't be a leader unless you sit in the saddle. I think he can." ●

Jeter tries to break up the double play, as future teammate Alex Rodriguez leaps over him.
(Barton Silverman/The New York Times)

When Jeter does what he did Tuesday, the Yankees simply nod their heads because they have come to expect amazing things from him.

On a Rainy Night, Jeter Lets the Sun Shine In

By JACK CURRY • Published: October 22, 2003

MIAMI, Wednesday, Oct. 22—Josh Beckett pumped a 97-mile-an-hour, shoulder-high fastball past Derek Jeter in the first inning, making him look uncomfortable and whiffing him on three pitches. But, when Jeter returned to the dugout, he spotted Luis Sojo, the coach in waiting, and made a bold prediction.

"He told me that he was going to get this guy," Sojo said. "He said, 'I'm going to kill him.' He did. He's amazing."

Jeter did. Jeter was amazing. He smacked three hits off Beckett, the only three the Yankees managed in seven and a third innings off him, and he started their first two rallies in a 6-1 victory over the Florida Marlins in Game 3 of the World Series at Pro Player Stadium on Tuesday. Because of Jeter's one-man show and Mike Mussina's dazzling pitching, the Yankees have a 2-1 lead in the four-of-seven-game series.

When Jeter was asked about his prediction, he smiled, stammered, looked away and finally admitted that he did tell Sojo that he would get Beckett.

Three solid hits and one huge victory later, Jeter playfully acted disappointed that Sojo had given away his secretive rant. "Well, I always say that," said Jeter, smiling again and scurrying away.

Twenty-seven men in black shorts, white shirts and black caps scampered around the wet field during a rain delay, and none of them were baseball players. They were the groundskeepers, who became very important people after a storm struck in the fifth inning and turned the World Series into the Soggy Series.

When play resumed, Mussina and Beckett continued pitching and both teams wound up playing through some more rain. Both teams were forced to act like excitable 8-year-olds on a hot day as they frolicked in the rain. No one frolicked as successfully as Jeter, who is two victories away from his fifth World Series ring in eight major league seasons.

"You can't explain it," Sojo said. "He's the best. We got Mr. Reggie Jackson around, and he's Mr. October, but, to me, Jeter is the real Mr. October."

"To me," said Luis Soto, "Jeter is the real Mr. October." (Barton Silverman/The New York Times)

"The leader of it all for the Yankees is Jeter," Jackson has said. "He's the guy who plays every day, he's the guy who makes the plays and he's the guy who gives people confidence."

When Jeter does what he did Tuesday, the Yankees simply nod their heads because they have come to expect amazing things from him. He is a very good player during the regular season who becomes a great player during the postseason. Jackson said Jeter is one of the most relaxed players he has ever seen in the postseason. Apparently, relaxing in the rain is one of Jeter's favorite pastimes.

"The leader of it all for the Yankees is Jeter," Jackson has said. "He's the guy who plays every day, he's the guy who makes the plays and he's the guy who gives people confidence."

In Game 3, Jeter gave the Yankees a chance against Beckett, who was throwing 97-m.p.h. fastballs, 87-m.p.h. changeups and 80-m.p.h. curveballs. One Yankees player said the Yankees could devastate the Marlins by winning Game 3 because Beckett has been their best pitcher and, if he lost, the Marlins might doubt their ability to rebound.

"If we beat them tonight, we've beaten their big guy," the player said. "That's something that will stay with them."

Sojo added: "We've got the confidence now. I don't think we're going to blow this."

After Beckett struck out Jeter in the first, Jeter said the only adjustment he made was telling himself not to swing at another high pitch and to make Beckett, a right-hander, bring the ball down in the strike zone.

It worked. The rest of the Yankees were 0 for 22 off Beckett. By the way, Beckett has allowed six hits in his last 20 postseason innings and the scorecard reads: Jeter 3, All the other hitters 3.

"When he gets to the postseason, he's going to bring it," said Willie Randolph, the third-base coach. "He's a special player and he knows what he has to do."

It only took Beckett 34 pitches to buzz past the first 10 batters and he was overpowering, but Jeter stroked a double to left field with one out in the fourth to give the Yankees their first hit. After a walk, a popout and a hit batter, Beckett walked Jorge Posada on a close 3-2 pitch to force home Jeter and tie the score, 1-1.

When Jeter batted in the eighth, Beckett was seeking his fourth straight strikeout. He was still throwing 97-m.p.h. fastballs, he was still dominating. Jeter, who knows he is producing when he smacks hits to the right side, reached out to slap an 0-1 pitch past first baseman Derrek Lee that rolled into the right-field corner. Why Lee was not playing closer to the line with the score tied late in the game is unknown. But Jeter, who slipped near first and barely touched the base, rumbled into second. Jeter scored on Hideki Matsui's two-out single, then pumped his fist after he scored, a sight that has become familiar for the Yankees. Just as familiar as Jeter doing something special to help the Yankees in the postseason. Rain, shine, anytime. ●

Mr. October Reggie Jackson and Mr. November Derek Jeter talk behind the batting cage before a game at Yankee Stadium. (Richard Perry/The New York Times)

All eyes are on Derek Jeter now that it is October and he is one of two shortstops still playing in North America.

Jeter Is Center of Attention, Especially in October

By GEORGE VECSEY • Published: October 23, 2003

All eyes are on Derek Jeter. Heads turn as he walks through the basement of the ballpark with giant ice packs on both shoulders.

Women stare at the ice packs as he heads toward the media interview room, with a walk somewhere between a saunter and a swagger.

"Maybe it's the green eyes, something a woman usually likes," one new Jeter fan wrote in an e-mail message, comparing Jeter to Salvatore Schillaci, who is known as Toto and is her favorite Italian soccer player from the 1990 World Cup.

All eyes are on Derek Jeter, but last night was not one of his finer games. He hit into two double plays as the Yankees lost to the Marlins, 4-3 in 12 innings, to tie the World Series at two games apiece.

Roger Clemens got to pitch again last night, most likely for the last time in his career. He had one bad inning, the first, then left with a strikeout in the seventh inning, to an impressive standing ovation, including the Marlins' dugout.

The Yankees would not have been here except for Jeter's performance in the seventh game of the American League Championship Series. With the Yankees trailing Pedro Martínez by three runs, Jeter whacked a double off the wall and reached second base and clapped his hands, in joy and in anticipation. More was coming, his body language told us.

All eyes are on Derek Jeter now that it is October and he is one of two shortstops still playing in North America.

The poor fellow. All we heard this past summer, as we kept a vague tab on the long baseball season, was that Derek Jeter had found his level. Limited power. Limited range. And perhaps even slightly passé in the new century of the slugger shortstop.

Ah, yes, we heard those bleats, quite often emanating from Yankees fans themselves, morbidly fearful that somehow a 39th pennant was impossible because Jeter would not slug 40 home runs or steal 40 bases.

Since then, we have seen Tejada pull a rock on the basepaths in the first round. We

Jeter dives for a ball in the 2003 American League Championship Series against the Boston Red Sox. (Vincent Laforet/The New York Times)

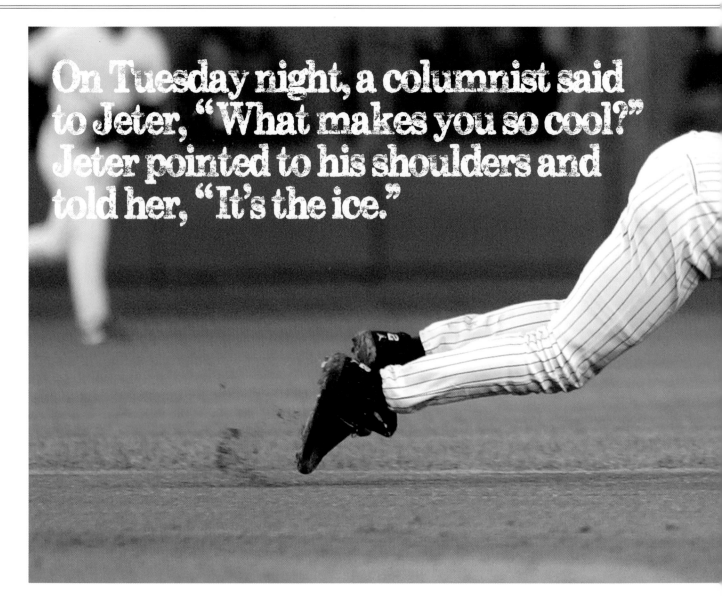

On Tuesday night, a columnist said to Jeter, "What makes you so cool?" Jeter pointed to his shoulders and told her, "It's the ice."

have seen Nomar blow hot and cold in the A.L.C.S. And here was Derek Jeter, standing on second base, clapping his hands.

All eyes are on Derek Jeter. In the commercial for a credit card, Mister Bluster demands to know if Jeter is running around at night, and Jeter says "absolutely not," and everybody knows he is fudging, but it's all right because he is so, how else can one put this, cute.

This spring, the Boss went off on one of his cruel and irrational tirades, picking on his leader, his best player, his most solid citizen. Jeter shrugged off the foolishness, and the Boss named Jeter captain, which, of course, Jeter had been, unofficially, all along. Then they starred together in the commercials that referred to George Steinbrenner's loose-cannon comments.

It really must be nice to be Derek Jeter.

All eyes are on Derek Jeter. On Tuesday night, young Josh Beckett blasted through the first 10 Yankees batters. Then Jeter lashed a double into the left-field corner. Once again, in the center of the field, he was the platoon leader waving his hand over his head to signal, "Follow me!" He added two hits and scored three runs.

Last night was a different story. Jeter went 1 for

Jeter dives to stop a grounder up the middle in the 2003 division series against the Minnesota Twins. (Barton Silverman/The New York Times)

6 and even made a sloppy tag that did not cost the Yankees. He's not perfect. But the Yankees will count on him as this Series comes down to its final innings.

Last night, Joe Torre described how he finally got to meet Tiger Woods, the golfer known for his own implacable excellence.

"I looked in his eyes and I saw Derek Jeter," Torre said.

Jeter has been dominating this team game for eight seasons. He has become a wise old hand, who welcomes the pressure of the World Series, saying, "I grew up with this." He hears the Boss has been quoting Patton or MacArthur or Lombardi about victory once again, and he says, "You know, this is not the first time I have heard this."

All eyes are on Derek Jeter. My soccer friend has been watching the World Series. She says her feelings for Jeter are purely maternal.

"So I've joined the ranks of the thousands of screaming teenagers, and the unknown number of women who feel as I do, women of all ages, I'm sure, and now I'm watching the World Series," my friend writes.

Now the World Series will definitely return from the comfortable and friendly Marlins stadium to the cramped and hostile Yankee Stadium. The Yankees will need a serious contribution from Jeter to ward off this low-budget but high-energy team. They will need Jeter standing on second base, clapping his hands, after a big hit.

On Tuesday night, a columnist said to Jeter, "What makes you so cool?" Jeter pointed to his shoulders and told her, "It's the ice." ●

"We have, arguably, the best left side of the infield in the history of baseball, and this is what it's going to be: Derek Jeter at shortstop, Alex Rodriguez at third base."

Yanks Assure Jeter He's Safe At Shortstop

By TYLER KEPNER • Published: February 17, 2004

Derek Jeter worked out yesterday in Tampa, Fla., and he will be in the Bronx today to welcome Alex Rodriguez to the Yankees. George Steinbrenner, the team's principal owner, told Jeter to go, and Jeter was apparently happy to do so. Jeter's fixation on winning rivals that of Steinbrenner, and the arrival of Rodriguez, the consensus best player in baseball, should keep the Yankees winning for years.

Rodriguez officially became the crown jewel of Steinbrenner's glittering collection yesterday when Commissioner Bud Selig approved the trade that sent Alfonso Soriano and a player to be named to the Texas Rangers for Rodriguez and $67 million. But while Rodriguez is the most talented, the team stressed yesterday that Jeter still has the most clout.

Steinbrenner and General Manager Brian Cashman have both spoken to Jeter to assure him he will stay at shortstop, even though Rodriguez has won two Gold Gloves there and Jeter has none. On a conference call yesterday, Cashman essentially roped off the area around shortstop and put up a "Keep Out" sign for Rodriguez.

"I'd like to take this time, for the organization, to put this all to rest right now," Cashman said. "This move would not have happened unless Alex Rodriguez moved to third base. Otherwise, we wouldn't even consider it. There is no issue, there is no 'who's the starting quarterback?' here.

"We have, arguably, the best left side of the infield in the history of baseball, and this is what it's going to be: Derek Jeter at shortstop, Alex Rodriguez at third base. And I think New York Yankees fans are going to be excited."

Selig does not share the enthusiasm. The $67 million is by far the most money ever included in a trade, and Selig seemed chagrined to endorse the deal.

"I am very concerned about the large amount of cash consideration involved in the transaction, and the length of time over which the cash is being paid," he said in a

Derek Jeter helps Alex Rodriguez put on the pinstripes for the first time at A-Rod's introductory press conference. (Barton Silverman/The New York Times)

"I'm delighted that Alex really wanted to be a Yankee and to play side by side with our team captain, Derek Jeter, who has shown himself to be a tremendous leader both on and off the field," Steinbrenner said in his statement

statement. "I want to make it abundantly clear to all clubs that I will not allow cash transfers of this magnitude to become the norm. However, given the unique circumstances, including the size, length and complexity of Mr. Rodriguez's contract and the quality of the talent moving in both directions, I have decided to approve the transaction."

Of Selig, one major league official said: "This is a killer for him. He understands that a lot of people—the Rangers, Rodriguez and other people—benefit from it. But what it does to the salary structure is just devastating to him, having one team $60 or $70 million higher than everybody else."

The Yankees are assuming seven years and $112 million for Rodriguez, and Randy Levine, the team president, said that for this season, they would spend no more with Rodriguez than they had budgeted. "It's close, on a cash basis, to neutral for us," Levine said.

That was a clear signal that the Yankees intend to cut third baseman Aaron Boone, who tore his anterior cruciate ligament playing basketball last month. The team would save about $4.8 million with that move, as well as the $5.4 million it owed Soriano and the $4 million Drew Henson forfeited by jumping to football. The Yankees will pay $14 million this season to Rodriguez, who is deferring $1 million.

"It's easy to scapegoat the Yankees," Levine said. "It's easy to deflect away by blaming the Yankees. The fact of the matter is, we do, under Mr. Steinbrenner's leadership, take bold actions, because that's his commitment to the fans."

In a statement, Steinbrenner hailed the move while making clear that his expectations are high.

"We are bringing to New York one of the premier players in the history of the game," Steinbrenner

said. "But, as I have always said, the way New Yorkers back us, we have to produce for them. The Yankees are in the toughest division in baseball and now, with the team we have assembled, we have to go out and produce on the field."

Steinbrenner resisted the urge to needle the Boston Red Sox, who traded for Rodriguez in December before the players union rejected the deal, believing the Red Sox had reduced the value of Rodriguez's contract.

"I know Larry Lucchino's disappointed," Levine said, referring to the Red Sox' president, a bitter adversary of Steinbrenner's. "We all understand that. They are a great organization, but this day is about the Yankees."

A baseball official said Lucchino contacted several people in the commissioner's office on Saturday asking about the Yankees' deal. Lucchino has credited the Yankees for their aggressiveness in landing Rodriguez, but he has stressed that it was a deal only they could pull off.

"I don't think he's angry at the Yankees for using their treasury," said Charles Steinberg, the Red Sox executive vice president for public affairs. "But you've got to describe why one deal happens and the other doesn't."

Cashman said he floated the idea of trading for Rodriguez in a conversation with Rangers General Manager John Hart early last week about third baseman Mike Lamb. Hart resisted, but later learned that Rodriguez would be willing to move to third for the Yankees. Rodriguez had decided this with his agent, Scott Boras, who told the Rangers' owner, Tom Hicks.

The deal was always Soriano for Rodriguez, but the Yankees initially wanted to pay only $90 million of the $179 million remaining on Rodriguez's contract. Texas wanted the Yankees to pay $112 million, a gap the Yankees made up eagerly. "Third base is a harder

position to fill than second base," Cashman said. "Soriano is a terrific player, and Alex is a great player. Soriano is a great player in his own right, but we found a third baseman in Alex who provides a lot more."

Cashman could pursue a second baseman in a trade—Baltimore's Jerry Hairston is available—but he said there was no urgency to look beyond Miguel Cairo and Enrique Wilson.

Rodriguez, who will wear No. 13, has played 1,267 career games at shortstop and none at third base. Cashman said the former Yankee third baseman Graig Nettles would assist Rodriguez in spring training. "I'm delighted that Alex really wanted to be a Yankee and to play side by side with our team captain, Derek Jeter,

who has shown himself to be a tremendous leader both on and off the field," Steinbrenner said in his statement.

He also told The Associated Press that the deal ranked with the free-agent acquisition of Reggie Jackson in 1976, and said: "Jeter is the captain. He is the leader."

One act of leadership will come at Yankee Stadium today, when Jeter will probably smile, throw an arm around Rodriguez and say all the right things. If Jeter looks secure, that is just how the Yankees want it. Shortstop is still his.

"You go with the man who brought you to the dance, and you stick with him," Cashman said. "Derek Jeter continues to get us to the dance. You don't mess with success." ●

The Yankee captain in a familiar flying formation. (Barton Silverman/The New York Times)

"**This was the most exciting game**
Yankees' principal owner, George

Jeter Gives Another Clinic in Leadership

By TYLER KEPNER • Published: July 3, 2004

Paul Quantrill faced Derek Jeter for years when he pitched for the Toronto Blue Jays, and he quickly developed his own scouting report. The reports Quantrill read suggested that Jeter was vulnerable to inside pitches, because of the way he dives across the plate. But Quantrill found that Jeter could handle any pitch and, even more dangerously, could adapt to any situation.

"The scouting reports could do this and do that," said Quantrill, now a teammate of Jeter's on the Yankees. "But he's a player that I categorize — and there aren't many guys like this — as a guy who will do what it takes for the team to win, to beat you, so you'd better be careful. He's not the guy you want up, because he'll try to do whatever it takes to win the games."

It seems so elementary, and to Jeter, it is. He is on the field to win, and he will adjust to the situation to meet that goal. Other hitters are more menacing, other fielders more sparkling, but few, if any, are as adaptable as Jeter.

Last week in Baltimore, he beat the Orioles with a home run over the center-field fence. He stole two bases in the Yankees' victory over Boston on Tuesday. On Wednesday night, he put down a crucial sacrifice bunt to help the Yankees win. Then came Thursday, when Jeter made a play that will likely be remembered for years in what was one of the most riveting games in memory.

"This was the most exciting game I have ever seen in all of sports," the Yankees' principal owner, George Steinbrenner, said in a statement, and the seminal moment belonged to Jeter, the captain, whom he called "an inspiration for all of our nation's youth."

There was Jeter, when the Yankees needed him most, making a play few shortstops could make. There was Jeter, with the game in the balance in the 12th inning against the Red Sox, sprinting and stretching and crashing into the stands, his face a wreck but Trot Nixon's fair ball nestled in his glove.

Jeter could have been a mother bird swooping for an egg falling from a nest. It was all instinct, the Yankees thought, something inside Jeter that few athletes possess.

"He knew, as he went after that ball, that he

Jeter shows off the bruises from his diving catch into the stands. (Keith Bedford/The New York Times)

have ever seen in all of sports," the Steinbrenner, said.

"He looked like he got hit by Mike Tyson," Rodriguez said.

had a decision to make," said Tony Clark, who watched the play unfold from first base. "Either you let the ball drop and try to minimize the damage, or you make the catch and pay the consequences. He knew that, no doubt about it, and he chose B."

Other shortstops could have gotten to the ball, Manager Joe Torre said. What separates Jeter is his utter disregard for his well-being.

"This kid is built this way," Torre said.

Alex Rodriguez, who followed Jeter into the stands and waved frantically for a trainer, said he would not have been surprised if Jeter had broken his jaw or separated his shoulder on the play.

"He looked like he got hit by Mike Tyson," Rodriguez said.

When Jeter emerged woozily from the stands, he had blood on his face, chin and jersey. But the consequences were not serious, considering the force of impact. Jeter left the game with a cut chin and bruises to his right cheek and right shoulder. He was at Columbia-Presbyterian Center of New York-Presbyterian Hospital when the Yankees came back to win, despite trailing by a run with two outs and no base runners in the 13th inning.

He was back in the lineup against the Mets last night, as he had promised teammate Jorge Posada he would be the night before.

Reporters swarmed Jeter's locker at Shea Stadium before the game last night, and the first question was, "What hurts?"

Jeter replied with the only answer he gives in these situations: "Nothing."

His face said otherwise. A dark red bruise covered the right side of Jeter's face, and he had two bandages

over his chin, which had received seven stitches.

But his vision was unimpaired, and that was all the Yankees had worried about. "I'm fine," Jeter insisted.

Jeter dislocated his left shoulder on opening night in Toronto last season, and he told Torre he could play the next game. He could not, of course; the injury cost him seven weeks. When he dashed for the ball on Thursday night, having shaded the pull-hitting Nixon up the middle, Jeter had the presence of mind to consider his shoulder.

"I tried to turn and jump to my right so I wouldn't hurt my left shoulder," he said.

Yankees General Manager Brian Cashman said the team would have been devastated to lose the game after Jeter's selflessness. Several teammates said they were inspired by Jeter's display, that it was the definition of his role as captain.

Who else would have attempted the play, knowing how badly he could have been hurt? "A utility player trying to stay in the league," Gary Sheffield said. "Those are probably the only guys."

There is more to Jeter's leadership style than the example he shows on the field. In the clubhouse and the dugout, Jeter seeks out teammates, casually asking if everything is O.K., letting them know he is available to talk.

Tom Gordon, a reliever in his first year with the Yankees, said it was obvious how much Jeter cared.

"I was with the White Sox last year, and if you had to call a guy a captain, you would probably call Frank Thomas one," Gordon said. "It's totally different between Derek Jeter and Frank Thomas. I don't want to say why, but it's night and day, you can say that. I was with the Cubs and Sammy Sosa — night and day."

"All three of those guys are great players. But from what I've seen of Derek Jeter, Derek Jeter is a captain of a ball club."

Few major league teams formally name a captain; there is no letterman's jacket in baseball, no sweater with a "C" stitched near the shoulder. Quantrill dismissed the idea of a team captain when he joined the Yankees, but he quickly came to see that the title suited Jeter.

"It's the real deal," Quantrill said. "He carries himself the right way. On the field, I've seen it for years playing against him. Off the field, Derek's very in tune with who he is, as a Yankee. He's very aware and cognizant of what the media sees, but he still is Derek. He's very approachable, he's one of the guys, but he's a rock star."

Even when Jeter was a 21-year-old rookie on the 1996 championship team, Torre said, veterans looked to him for guidance. The Yankees invested $189 million in Jeter when they signed him to a 10-year contract after the 2000 season, and they proceeded with the Rodriguez trade in February only after Rodriguez agreed to give up shortstop and move to third base, never mind his two Gold Gloves at shortstop.

Rodriguez played an inning at his former position after Jeter's catch Thursday, and never had the position seemed more like Jeter's. If it looked odd to see Rodriguez there, it felt strange to him, too, he said.

This is Jeter's team, now more than ever.

"When it's all said and done, Derek is going to be one of the greatest shortstops ever to play the game," Rodriguez said. "And maybe one of the biggest winners ever." ●

Jeter dives into the stands to catch a fly ball in the 12th inning against the Boston Red Sox on July 1, 2004. (AP Photo/Frank Franklin II)

"You don't know what's going to happen, catcher Jorge Posada said. "You don't know what people are made of until it's said and done."

If It's October, It Must Be Jeter Time

By Tyler Kepner • Published: October 8, 2004

MINNEAPOLIS, Oct. 7 — All these years, Derek Jeter has been kidding. There is a statistic that matters to him. A few years ago, Jeter told Luis Sojo that one number drives him.

"The only thing he likes is scoring runs," said Sojo, a former Yankees infielder who now coaches third base. "He doesn't worry about anything else. The one specific number that does inspire him is 100 runs, because he knows that if he scores 100 runs, we have a chance to win 100 games."

It is typical of Jeter, who never complicates a task. The team with the most runs wins, so he may as well try to score.

This single-minded passion fueled Jeter's dash for the plate in the 12th inning on Wednesday at Yankee Stadium. When he slid in safely, he brought the Yankees here for Game 3 of their best-of-five-game division series with the Minnesota Twins tied at one game apiece.

That is how the series stood last October before the Yankees throttled the Twins in Games 3 and 4 behind Roger Clemens and David Wells. This time, the Yankees turn to

Kevin Brown on Friday and probably Javier Vazquez on Saturday. Neither has pitched for them before in the playoffs.

"You don't know what's going to happen," catcher Jorge Posada said. "You don't know what people are made of until it's said and done."

For all of their uncertainties, the Yankees still have Jeter, and that is sometimes enough to carry them. It should not be this way in baseball.

In his prime with the Seattle Mariners, Ken Griffey Jr. once explained his limitations in simple terms: "I bat third." In other words, no matter how good any player may be, he bats only once every nine times. By the rules, his contributions are limited.

Jeter, somehow, defies that. Over his nine-year major league career, his postseason batting average is .313, 2 points lower than his regular-season average. But every night in the postseason, he seems to have a defining moment.

"You saw it last night," Sojo said Thursday. "Every day, he comes up with something good."

In some ways, Wednesday's game belonged

Every night in the postseason, Jeter seems to have a defining moment. (Barton Silverman/The New York Times)

to Alex Rodriguez, who went 4 for 6 with a home run and the tying double in the 12th. But it was a tour de force for Jeter, who showed off all the ways he can beat a team.

"He's capable of doing so many things," closer Mariano Rivera said. "He can do it many ways: with the home run, with the steal, with the bunt. He's always there. Always there."

When Jeter stepped in against Brad Radke to lead off the bottom of the first, the Yankees had not scored in 18 postseason innings. Jeter crushed a pitch into the black seats in center field. No Yankee had sent a ball there in the postseason since Reggie Jackson in the 1977 World Series.

"We certainly needed a lift, especially with Minnesota scoring a run in the top of the first," Manager Joe Torre said. "He hit a ball to Reggieland. That's not really part of his signature, but he made a statement there."

In the fifth inning, Jeter fielded a chopper over the middle, stepped on second and fired to first for a double play, erasing the Twins' leadoff base runner. In the seventh, he sacrificed Miguel Cairo to second so Rodriguez could drive him in with a single.

Cairo missed a crucial sacrifice bunt in the Yankees' loss in Game 1, striking out before Jeter bounced into a double play. It was a subtle error by Cairo, but it contributed to the 2-0 loss.

Jeter's bunt on Wednesday was just as subtle and just as pivotal. This season he had 16 sacrifices, double his career high, taking advantage of the firepower behind him in Rodriguez and Gary Sheffield. Now, he may bunt even more.

"Early in the year it might depend on who you're facing or if you're not feeling as good," Jeter said. "Now, I don't really care. We're just trying to score runs. I don't care how I feel."

With one out in the 12th and Cairo on first, Jeter took four straight balls from Joe Nathan, the tiring Twins closer. Rodriguez's double tied the score and moved Jeter to third. Sheffield was walked intentionally.

Sojo approached Jeter during a pitching change and reminded him of the basics.

"I told him, 'Ground ball, we have to go; fly ball, I'll let you know,'" Sojo said. "He said, 'You don't have to let me know anything; I'm going to go no matter what.'"

The Twins moved the outfielders in, and Hideki Matsui ripped a liner to Jacque Jones in right. Jones caught the ball flat-footed and did not anticipate that Jeter would tag up.

"I don't know why," Jeter said. "Probably because he caught it at second base."

Jeter, the Yankees' captain, was undaunted. Instead of breaking for home on the liner, he broke back to third, putting himself in position to tag up. Most runners would be halfway down the base line. Jeter's reaction was pure instinct, and he beat the relay throw.

"That's the way he plays baseball," Cairo said. "His head is into the game from beginning to end, and there's not too many guys that play that way. He never takes his mind off the game."

It is October, and Jeter's mind keeps it simple. Score runs. Keep the other team from scoring. Win the game, always.

"I don't see a better player than that guy in October," Sojo said. "The things that he does, it's unbelievable. Thank God he's on our side." ●

Jeter after scoring the winning run in the 12th inning of Game 2 of the 2004 division series against the Twins. (Vincent Laforet/The New York Times)

Jeter's reaction to his accomplishment was nonchalant. He doffed his batting helmet to acknowledge the fans, who were chanting his name. And then he took a lead at second.

Jeter Beats Out a Milestone

By KAREN CROUSE • Published: May 27, 2006

The night was damp, the Yankees' opponent was doleful, the holiday getaway traffic was dispiriting. The reason why 48,035 fans braved gloomy skies, gridlock and the Kansas City Royals last night became as clear as an indelible memory when Derek Jeter, the Yankees shortstop, led off the fourth inning against Royals starter Scott Elarton.

Popping flashbulbs blazed Jeter's path from the on-deck circle to home plate, as if he were a leading man at a red-carpet premiere. The Yankees were down by three runs, and the fans were up on their feet cheering. It was Jeter the fans came to see, and he would not disappoint them.

He hit a dribbler, the ball traveling three feet but proving to be such a big hit that a rain delay in the ninth inning could not dampen the crowd's spirits, nor could the fact that the Washington Generals of major-league baseball were leading the Yankees by 7-5 at the time of the delay.

Paul Bako, the Royals' catcher, fielded Jeter's ball, but his throw to first sailed over the head of Doug Mientkiewicz, allowing Jeter to take second. After a dramatic pause, the official ruling came down from on high: The official scorer in the press box awarded Jeter a hit and charged Bako with an error. So it was that Jeter became the eighth Yankee to reach 2,000 hits, joining Lou Gehrig, Babe Ruth, Mickey Mantle, Bernie Williams, Joe DiMaggio, Don Mattingly and Yogi Berra.

In the home dugout, the players draped themselves over the railing like bunting and applauded Jeter. From their vantage point, his accomplishment looked less like a milestone than a stepping stone toward what is considered perhaps his ultimate destiny: becoming the first player wearing Yankee pinstripes to reach 3,000 hits.

"Oh yeah, he can get to 3,000" said Williams, the right fielder who recorded his 2,000th hit in 2004. "He's still has a lot of career ahead of him, you know. He's just breezing through this."

Jeter's reaction to his accomplishment was nonchalant. He doffed his batting helmet to

Jeter beats out a dribbler to record his 2,000th career hit. (John Dunn/The New York Times)

acknowledge the fans, who were chanting his name. And then he took a lead at second. His muted reaction was predictable. Indeed, Yankees Manager Joe Torre called it before the game.

Asked to imagine what would happen if Jeter picked up his 2000th hit, Torre said, "I don't think he'd be comfortable having anyone pay attention to it." He added, "I think he's just going to say, 'Let's get on with the show.'"

Jeter conveyed that sentiment by stealing third on the first pitch that Elarton threw to the next batter, Gary Sheffield. He would end up scoring on Alex Rodriguez's single.

"Two-thousand hits, 31 years old," Torre said. "That's not bad. It's pretty impressive how consistent he has been for 10 years. Everybody is hoping he stays healthy, so he can get to that next level."

Jeter said he does not pay attention to individual statistics, that the only thing he cares about is winning. Williams is convinced that is true, but he also believes

this: "I think he has a side of him that he doesn't really show anybody.

"I'm thinking in some ways he's reluctant to show somewhat his human side. I think the expectations are so big on him to lead this club on a mental level, on a performance level, on a physical level, that I think he feels he needs to put almost a superhuman shield on."

The shield was firmly in place when Jeter was asked about the prospect of reaching 3,000 hits. "That is a long, long, long ways away," he said.

Maybe 2,000 hits is not a huge accomplishment in baseball. But there was a sense in Yankee Stadium last night that in celebrating what Jeter did, people were celebrating the person as much as the player.

Torre noted how rare Jeter's humility is in baseball.

"Because we champion these kinds of things," Torre said. "It seems like individual achievements are what we make a big fuss about. It's really tough to not have that be the most important thing." ●

Opposite: "Two thousand hits, 31 years old," said Joe Torre. "That's not bad." Here Jeter watches the action with Torre, Don Zimmer, and Mel Stottlemyre. Above: Jeter makes a play at second. (Both photos: Barton Silverman/The New York Times)

With Five-Hit Performance, Jeter Gains Entry Into an Elite Club

By JACK CURRY • Published: October 5, 2006

Mike Stanley was watching Derek Jeter's exploits Tuesday night when the broadcasters mentioned that Jeter had become the sixth player to have at least five hits in a postseason game. Stanley, another five-hit wonder, grew more interested in a game that had already intrigued him.

"When they started saying something about it, I said: That's me. That's me," Stanley said. "Of course, I was in a room by myself watching the game at 11:30."

Stanley's outburst did not wake anyone in his family, so he decided to wait until morning to tell his wife, Erin, that he and Jeter were now connected in playoff history. But she barely recalled the five hits he had when the Boston Red Sox destroyed the Cleveland Indians, 23-7, in an American League division series game in 1999.

"She said, 'Was that in that blowout game?'" Stanley said. "Some of my friends and close buddies might remember it. But mine weren't huge, important hits. Derek Jeter's were a lot grander."

Stanley was not the only person who was watching Jeter, a former teammate, duplicating his feat. Paul Molitor, the one player to have five hits in a World Series game, while he was with the Milwaukee Brewers in 1982, was also watching the game on TV.

Molitor stressed how difficult it was to have five hits in a game, never mind a playoff contest. Thousands of players have appeared in the postseason, but only six have recorded five hits. It is an elite club. As a comparison, five players have hit three homers in a playoff game.

"You can do the math," Molitor said. "With a lot of people, you think of the odds and what people hit, it's tough for anyone stringing together five hits in one game. Derek Jeter had a great game."

Hideki Matsui, Jeter's teammate and someone who had five hits in Game 3 of the 2004 A.L. Championship Series, had a dugout seat for Jeter's rampage. But that close proximity did not make him reflect on what he did against the Red Sox two years ago.

A bunt, home run or a single, Jeter will do whatever it takes. (Barton Silverman/The New York Times)

Jeter had a neat baseball moment on a Tuesday in October. Actually, he had five of them.

"I had no idea I was one of them," Matsui said. "In the playoffs, you don't remember what you did. It's what the team does."

Paul Blair, who had five hits for the Baltimore Orioles when they won the first A.L.C.S. in 1969, and Marquis Grissom, who had five hits for the Atlanta Braves in their 1995 National League division series, may or may not have been watching Jeter and the Yankees. Neither responded to a telephone message.

Until Tuesday, Grissom was the only player to go 5 for 5. But Jeter equaled that as the Yankees silenced the Detroit Tigers, 8-4, which was the tightest score for any of the five-hit games and heightened the importance of his performance.

Molitor's Brewers defeated the St. Louis Cardinals, 10-0, in Game 1 of that series. Matsui's Yankees hammered the Red Sox, 19-8. Blair's Orioles won, 11-2, over the Minnesota Twins, and Grissom's Braves beat the Colorado Rockies, 10-4.

When Stanley had five hits in a game Boston won by 16 runs, John Valentin went 4 for 5 with two homers and a double, driving in seven runs. Stanley said his own performance deserved to be a five-hit footnote. Stanley, no speedster, recalled how he had a swinging bunt for a single, but he had forgotten that he also hit a triple.

"Me, being known for my wheels, I guess that game epitomized my career," Stanley said.

Molitor is the only Hall of Famer among the group, although Jeter may eventually join him there. Even though Molitor stressed how arduous it was to have one hit after another until reaching five in the same game, he also said that a player who had filled his mind with four positive images could convince himself that there should be a fifth.

"A lot of times when I had four hits, I felt really good about the fifth one," said Molitor, who had 3,319 career hits.

"You're not seeing the players. You're seeing a lot of open field, as opposed to when you're struggling, when it seems like there's 25 guys out there."

Stanley agreed with Molitor and said that Jeter's final at-bat, in which he homered to center field off Jamie Walker, was an example of that confidence.

"He got fooled on a curveball, and he was able to stay back and hit it out," Stanley said. "That's being completely locked in."

As Molitor jogged out for the ninth inning of his memorable game 24 years ago, he saw a message on the scoreboard noting that he was the first player with five hits in a World Series game. Molitor remembered it as "a neat baseball moment." Jeter had a neat baseball moment on a Tuesday in October. Actually, he had five of them. ●

A Jeter fan displays her affection. (Chang W. Lee/The New York Times)

For superstitious reasons, Jeter does not like talking about hot streaks as they happen. But when he stays in one all season, it is sometimes hard to avoid.

Jeter Sees Sunshine Amid Clouds

By TYLER KEPNER • Published: May 13, 2007

SEATTLE, May 12 — Most days, a few hours before the Yankees play, Derek Jeter will stroll into the clubhouse sipping a grande cappuccino from Starbucks. No endorsements, though; Starbucks does not need a pitchman, and he already hawks Gatorade and Propel fitness water.

Three hours before Friday night's game, Jeter stood in the middle of the visiting locker room at Safeco Field with a different kind of treat: a soft-serve ice cream cone from the players' lounge. As an accessory, it made him look carefree, which in many ways he is.

"You can tell he enjoys every aspect of the game," said first baseman Doug Mientkiewicz, who is playing on a team with Jeter for the first time this season. "The good, the bad and the ugly, he thoroughly enjoys all of it."

For the Yankees this season, there have been plenty of bad and ugly. But aside from a brief fielding slump in early April, not much of it has been caused by Jeter. He leads the American League in batting average (.376) and hits (53), maintaining a sunny outlook despite the Yankees' erratic start.

That part comes easy to Jeter, the team captain, who said he always tried to take the long view, and the positive one.

"I'm optimistic by nature," Jeter said. "Even when things are going poorly, you've got to find something positive. You have to. Because if you get caught up in being negative all the time, you'll never get out of any kind of funk."

Jeter is not immune to slumps, of course. He went 0 for 32 early in the 2004 season, and when Mientkiewicz struggled in April, Jeter often reminded him of his own slow starts.

But he has been remarkably consistent over the past two seasons. At one point, from Aug. 20, 2006, through May 3, he had at least one hit in 59 of 61 games. The stretch began with a 25-game hitting streak, followed by a hitless game.

Jeter getting ready for batting practice. (Richard Perry/The New York Times)

A 14-game hitting streak followed that. Then, after another hitless game, Jeter ripped off 20 in a row.

According to Trent McCotter of the Society for American Baseball Research, only one other player since 1900 had as many as 59 games out of 61 with a hit: Joe DiMaggio, who hit safely in 60 of 61 in 1941, when he had a record 56-game streak.

For superstitious reasons, Jeter does not like talking about hot streaks as they happen. But when he stays in one all season, it is sometimes hard to avoid.

"I don't think about it, really," he said. "All I try to do, pretty much, is to be consistent. I don't try to overanalyze anything, I don't try to sit back and say, You're doing this or that. I just try to consistently help out every day.

"You look at it that way, especially when things are going bad, you're able to get out of it, because you're not concerning yourself with how you're doing individually."

In a short time around Jeter, Mientkiewicz already understands the essence of what makes him succeed. Mientkiewicz said it was obvious to him that Jeter kept everything simple and took each at-bat with a clear head, never letting one plate appearance affect the next.

As a hitter, Jeter reminds Mientkiewicz of the Hall of Famer Paul Molitor, his former teammate with the Minnesota Twins. Both are exceptional hitters who make their own luck.

"He's got that Paul Molitor knack," Mientkiewicz said. "Even in batting practice, Molly never hit a ball right to the shortstop or right to the second baseman. They always had that knack of always hitting the ball where somebody wasn't.

"Tony Gwynn had it, too — they just find holes. When he rolls a ball over, it's never right to somebody.

Then he tops one off the plate, and it's right in front of the plate and he beats it out. Then he barrels it up and hits it 440 in the gap, and it's a homer."

There is a tendency toward hyperbole when discussing any hot hitter, and Jeter is no exception. But history shows that he does not vary much from the way he starts a season. Only once has Jeter's season-ending batting average been more than .013 below his average May 11. And that year (1999), he finished second in the league in hitting at .349.

Jeter is now batting third, behind the struggling Bobby Abreu, because Manager Joe Torre said he felt more comfortable with Jeter in a position to drive in runs.

"He's gotten an awful lot of two-out hits," Torre said. "That's the bonus, as far as I'm concerned. Yeah, man on third base, less than two out, you're supposed to knock in the run. But with two out, that's what turns into a great at-bat. When you get two-out R.B.I.'s, that's something that really deflates the opposition and perks up your team."

With two outs and runners in scoring position, Jeter had a .600 average through Friday, with nine hits in 15 at-bats. It does not always work this way, but for now Jeter is living up to his reputation of giving the team what it needs. He said he was not thinking of anything else.

"When the season's over, you get a chance to reflect on what happened during the season," Jeter said. "Once you sit around and start talking about what you've done, that's when you're in trouble. You always strive to do something better." ●

A fan screams for Jeter. (Barton Silverman/The New York Times)

"He stunk," Ledee said. "In the beginning, he stunk."

In Beginning, Even Jeter Doubted Jeter

By JACK CURRY • Published: June 18, 2007

This was before the 2,242 hits, before the four World Series rings, before he became the captain of the Yankees and before he attracted comparisons to Joe DiMaggio. This was Derek Jeter in Tampa, Fla., 15 years ago. This was Jeter's first day playing professionally for the Yankees.

Ricky Ledee was there starting for Class A Tampa, waiting to see the first-round draft choice who would immediately become the starting shortstop. Ledee's first impression of Jeter was that he was really skinny. Ledee held up his left pinky to show how thin he thought Jeter looked as an 18-year-old.

Jeter teased Ledee, his former minor league and major league teammate, behind the batting cage before the Yankees silenced the Mets, 8-2, at Yankee Stadium last night. Jeter is still playing shortstop for the Yankees while Ledee, who helped the Yankees win two titles, is hanging on with the Mets, his seventh team.

Jeter singled in the first inning off Orlando Hernández and trotted home on Alex Rodriguez's two-run homer. Once again, Jeter did something, even if it was a little something, to aggravate the Mets. Ledee did not play in the three-game series.

Every time Ledee shared a memory about Jeter, he stressed that he revered him.

Still, Ledee, the journeyman outfielder who never fulfilled his promise with the Yankees, smiled when he discussed the early days of watching a raw Jeter, the player who has developed into an icon here.

"He stunk," Ledee said. "In the beginning, he stunk."

Reminded of the beginning, Jeter acknowledged that, for a while, he did stink. In Jeter's debut, he went 0 for 7 with five strikeouts in a doubleheader and also made a throwing error that lost one of the games. Jeter, who had only one strikeout in 59 at-bats in his senior year in high school, was exasperated after several hours as a Yankee.

A former teammate who reveres Jeter recalls some bumpy early days. (Chip Litherland/The New York Times)

"I think I was 0 for 8 with seven strikeouts," said Jeter, who embellished it into an even worse day.

"I think I was 0 for 8 with seven strikeouts," said Jeter, who embellished it into an even worse day.

Maybe Jeter exaggerated because the first bad day bled into a second and a third; Jeter did not get a hit until his 15th at-bat.

Ledee said Jeter was so flummoxed as a hitter that simply putting the ball in play was an accomplishment. Was this the talented player from Kalamazoo, Mich., the Yankees gave an $800,000 signing bonus?

"It was bad," Ledee said. "The first couple of days were tough."

The first time Jeter met his teammates at a Gulf Coast League game, he was driven there by a Yankees executive.

Ledee, who had taken the one-hour bus ride with the team, said some players grumbled about how the new player had received preferential treatment.

Ledee said they were moaning even more once Jeter actually played a day later.

"First, he didn't travel with us," Ledee said. "Then, in the first game, he blew the game. We were like, 'He got all that money?' It was rookie league stuff."

Statistically, Jeter did struggle with his first minor league team. He hit .202 with 3 homers, 25 runs batted in and 12 errors in 47 games. Ledee, who batted only .229 in his third stint at Tampa, said Jeter's first hit was a bloop single to right field.

But while Jeter looked overwhelmed, Ledee said the skinny prospect had skills. Ledee explained how minor leaguers never know if they are going to make it to the majors, so they study everyone around them as if they are competitors. When teammates analyzed the young Jeter, Ledee said they spotted someone who was soon going to handle Class A and keep advancing. Jeter made it to the majors in 1995 and was with the Yankees for good by 1996.

"You could see that everything was there," Ledee said. "The bat speed was there. He stayed inside the ball and hit the ball the other way. The Jeter that I see now, he was the same then."

Ledee said that he never saw Jeter get depressed about his problems. No matter how much Jeter struggled, Ledee said he stayed focused.

"You don't know if, in his room, he was fighting himself," Ledee said. "But, on the field, you never saw that."

While Jeter made sure that no one saw him sweat, he did have some long nights when he returned to the Radisson Bay Harbor Inn in Tampa. Jeter sat on the balcony and watched the cars breeze by, anything to take his mind off his troubles.

"Back in the hotel, I might have gotten down," Jeter said. "But not in front of anybody."

Fifteen years later, Jeter is one of the leading hitters in the American League. Ledee said he played with many minor leaguers who had better starts than Jeter, but none who have had the kind of finish that Jeter is fashioning. ●

Fans model Jeter's jersey. (Fred R. Conrad/The New York Times)

UNITED STATES TAKES BACK THE RYDER CUP

Phil Mickelson and his wife, Amy, flashed smiles from tee to green after the United States won the Ryder Cup for the first time since 1999, beating Europe, 16½-11½, in Louisville, Ky. Page D9.

GIANTS FIND A WAY TO STAY UNBEATEN

Fred Robbins and the Giants sacked Carson Palmer six times, but they needed John Carney's fourth field goal to beat the Bengals in overtime, 26-23. Page D7.

FAMILIAR SCENE IN METS' DUGOUT

Aaron Heilman was the last in a contingent of Mets relievers who allowed four runs in the final two innings of a 7-6 loss to the Braves in Atlanta. Page D4.

Sports Monday

□□N   D1

MONDAY, SEPTEMBER 22, 2008

The New York Times

A Long Goodbye To an 85-Year Run

Derek Jeter and the Yankees saluting the fans after winning the final game at Yankee Stadium. Jeter also took the microphone and praised the fans as the greatest in the world.

VINCENT LAFORET FOR THE NEW YORK TIMES

PHOTOGRAPHS BY BARTON SILVERMAN/THE NEW YORK TIMES

Bernie Williams waved to the crowd. Whitey Ford, at left in right photograph, and Don Larsen took dirt from the pitcher's mound during the pregame ceremony.

LEFT, NICK LAHAM/GETTY IMAGES; VINCENT LAFORET FOR THE NEW YORK TIMES

The final lineups, left. Fans peered at dusty handprints left on the outfield wall.

A Full House and a Crowded Stage Mark Yankee Stadium's Closing Night

By TYLER KEPNER

It will only grow with time, like Lou Gehrig's farewell, Don Larsen's masterpiece and Reggie Jackson's third home run in a World Series game. Untold thousands will say they were there the night the curtain fell on baseball's grandest stage.

| YANKEES | 7 |
| ORIOLES | 3 |

It happened Sunday night in the Bronx, when Yankee Stadium hosted a baseball game for the last time. It went out the way it opened, with a victory, this one over the Baltimore Orioles, 7-3. Babe Ruth hit the first home run, in 1923, and José Molina hit the last, a two-run shot to left that broke a tie in the fourth inning.

The Yankees held off elimination from playoff contention with the victory, the eighth in their final nine games at Yankee Stadium. Andy Pettitte, the winning pitcher, worked into the sixth inning, waving his cap to the fans who never stopped cheering until he took a curtain call.

Manager Joe Girardi compared it to the seventh game of the World Series, because the Yankees could not afford to lose, and it felt that way for many reasons. From the bunting along the upper deck, to the United States Army Field Band, to the mix of excitement and anxiety bubbling up in the guts of the uniformed Yankees, there was no doubt this night would be special.

"I feel as nervous as I was before a playoff game," said Bernie Williams, back in pinstripes at last, one of more than 20 former Yankees who re-

CHANG W. LEE/THE NEW YORK TIMES

José Molina watching his two-run homer off Chris Waters in the fourth inning. It was the final home run at Yankee Stadium.

Continued on Page D3

Jeter Thanks Fans in Speech After Game

By JACK CURRY • Published: September 22, 2008

The last game at Yankee Stadium was over, but the fans waited. There would never be another pitch thrown in this beautiful park, but the fans still waited. That was when Derek Jeter gathered his Yankees teammates, walked to the pitcher's mound, took a microphone and thanked them.

Jeter told the fans that it was an honor for the players to wear the Yankee uniform. Applause. He said the Yankees were about history, tradition and memories, and passing along the memories from generation to generation. Even more applause. Then Jeter told the last 54,610 people to sit in these blue seats that they were the greatest fans in the world. Deafening applause.

"I was scared to death," Jeter said. "When I was younger, I used to get nervous when I had to do an oral report in front of 25 people. I guess I've come a long way."

A few days ago, the Yankees asked Jeter, the team captain, if he would address the fans after Sunday's game. Jeter agreed, but he said he did not learn until before the game that he would actually be speaking. Manager Joe Girardi removed Jeter with two outs in the ninth inning so he could receive one final ovation.

"Two outs in the ninth, I thought, 'I better think of something,'" Jeter said.

Even though Jeter was offering his words to more than 54,000 fans, not the 25 he used to address in a classroom, he did not prepare.

"I didn't think about it," Jeter said. "I didn't know what I was going to say. I know I wanted to acknowledge the fans. If you ask me now what I said, I probably couldn't tell you."

But Jeter's words worked. Like Jeter's play, his speech was effective and classy. Even though Jeter went 0 for 5 in a 7-3 win over the Baltimore Orioles, the fans who adore him will remember his speech and not his hitless game.

"Derek said it with such eloquent words when he thanked the fans for their support," said Bernie Williams, the former Yankee who received the loudest pregame ovation.

After Jeter's speech, he led the Yankees on a lap around the Stadium in which the players thanked the fans some more. Because police officers in riot gear and officers on horseback were stationed around the Stadium, the players remained about 50 feet away from the fans. Still, it was a nice ending to the last night at the Stadium.

"This was perfect," Jeter said. "I don't know if I could use another adjective. It was perfect." ●

Sports Saturday

The New York Times

2,722

From Gehrig to Jeter, A Record Is Passed

With fans chanting his name, Derek Jeter waved his helmet toward the Yankee Stadium crowd and pointed to the box where his family was sitting.

RICHARD PERRY/THE NEW YORK TIMES

RAY STUBBLEBINE/REUTERS

Derek Jeter singling to right in the third inning to pass Lou Gehrig and become the Yankees' career hits leader.

By TYLER KEPNER

Derek Jeter grew up on Yankees history birth and by providence. He was nurtured as a by his grandmother, who lived in New Jersey, drafted into the tradition as a first-round pick 1992. Only a few years ago, though, did Jeter tice that nobody in his team's history had e reached 3,000 hits. Teammates stumbled on while paging through a record book.

"Then we were wondering who had most," Jeter said on Friday afternoon. "But it's like you sit there and target it."

For more than 70 years, Lou Gehrig had most hits for the franchise, a record that stood til Jeter passed him Friday with his 2,722nd hi single that skipped past Gehrig's old position, f base. Jeter's graceful grind through 15 seas has vaulted him past his storied predecessor team captain.

Jeter connected in the third inning, on a fastball from Chris Tillman of the Baltimore oles that got past the diving first baseman, L Scott. Jeter, who has made a career of hard balls to the opposite field, spread his arms w and clapped after rounding first base.

The players on the Yankees' bench pou from the dugout to greet him at first base, tak turns hugging him. Alex Rodriguez was the firs arrive, then Mark Teixeira, Joba Chamberla

Continued on Page D5

Applause Is Appropriate Response

Clap hands for Derek Jeter.

Clap hands, the way he does when he pulls into second base in the bottom of the ninth, star into the dugout with that grin of his.

Clap hands for Derek Jeter, breaking the record of Lou Gehrig for most hits by a Yankee.

Not just any franchise. The Yankees.

GEORGE VECSEY

SPORTS OF THE TIMES

Clap hands for Jeter, who is having the year of his life, swattin base hits and fielding his position, not that he will talk much about himself.

Raised right, the other day he said his paren gave him permission to put aside his captain per sona and, for a second or two, enjoy approachin Gehrig's record.

The record is important because the Yanke are — and recognize that this is coming from an old Brooklyn Dodgers fan — the great sports fra chise of America, in terms of championships and legends, never mind the Steelers and the Celtics and so on.

Jeter now has more hits as a Yankee than Ruth or Gehrig or DiMaggio or Mantle or Mattin ly or Williams, all those grand Yankees who nee no introduction. He has surpassed them in the summer he turned 35, still metaphorically divin

Continued on Page D5

"I never imagined, I never dreamt of this," Jeter said after midnight Saturday morning. "Your dream was always to play for the team. Once you get here, you just want to stay and try to be consistent."

Jeter Passes Gehrig as Yankees Hits Leader

By TYLER KEPNER • September 12, 2009

Derek Jeter grew up on Yankees history, by birth and by providence. He was nurtured as a fan by his grandmother, who lived in New Jersey, and drafted into the tradition as a first-round pick in 1992. Only recently, though, did Jeter learn that nobody had gathered 3,000 hits for his team.

Teammates stumbled on the fact while paging through a record book, and Jeter said they wondered who had the most. The record was clearly in Jeter's sights, but he never resolved to target Lou Gehrig, never made it a goal.

"I never imagined, I never dreamt of this," Jeter said after midnight Saturday morning. "Your dream was always to play for the team. Once you get here, you just want to stay and try to be consistent. So this really wasn't a part of it. The whole experience has been overwhelming."

On a drizzly Friday night at Yankee Stadium, Jeter's graceful grind through 15 seasons vaulted him past Gehrig, his storied predecessor as team captain. Gehrig held the record for more than 70 years, until Jeter's

2,722nd hit skipped past Gehrig's old position, first base, for a single.

Jeter connected in the third inning of a 10-4 loss to the Baltimore Orioles that was delayed at the start and again in the seventh inning. Jeter lashed a 2-0 fastball from Chris Tillman on a hop past the diving first baseman, Luke Scott. The hard-hit ball to opposite field is Jeter's signature hit, and he spread his arms wide and clapped after rounding first base.

The players on the Yankees' bench poured from the dugout to greet him, taking turns giving hugs. Alex Rodriguez was the first to arrive, before Robinson Cano, Mark Teixeira, Joba Chamberlain and the rest.

"I think you saw the closeness of the group," Manager Joe Girardi said. "Even the guys that have only been here for a year, they understood."

The fans chanted Jeter's first and last names, and Jeter waved his helmet to all corners of the new Yankee Stadium. As he did on Wednesday, when he tied the record, Jeter pointed to the box with his parents, sister and friends on the suite level above the Yankees' on-deck circle. Jeter's girlfriend, the actress Minka Kelly, stood beside his mother, Dorothy, and both smiled widely.

The crowd continued to chant for Jeter, and Nick Swisher, the next batter, stepped out of the box to make the moment last. As the cheers cascaded over Jeter, he waved his helmet again and then clapped a few times in Swisher's direction: back to work.

"The fans," Jeter said, when asked what he would remember most, years from now. "It wasn't ideal conditions tonight, and for the fans to stick around, it really means a lot. Since day one, they've always been very supportive. They're just as much a part of this as I am."

The hit arrived in Jeter's second at-bat against Tillman, a heralded Orioles rookie who challenged him with a 94 mile-an-hour pitch. Tillman had won their duel in the first inning, striking Jeter out with a curveball after getting ahead with fastballs.

It was raining then, a persistent, heavy mist swirling around the stadium, with standing pools of water on the warning track. The grounds crew hustled to rake the mound after the top of the first, and a double splashed in a mud puddle down the right field line in the second.

In the third inning, though, the rain tapered for a bit. In any case, the crowd of 46,771 did not seem to care. The fans stood for Jeter then, snapping photos of each pitch, and an inning later, commemorative T-shirts and pennants were on sale at stadium gift shops.

Principal owner George Steinbrenner was not there. His health has declined, and he has not been to a home game since opening day. But his publicist quickly issued a statement on his behalf.

"For those who say today's game can't produce legendary players, I have two words: Derek Jeter," Steinbrenner's statement said. "As historic and significant as becoming the Yankees' all-time hit leader

is, the accomplishment is all the more impressive because Derek is one of the finest young men playing the game today."

Jeter said Steinbrenner called him during the second rain delay, and that Steinbrenner had nice things to say. Jeter is a link to the owner's more visible, vigorous days, and he seemed touched that Steinbrenner reached out.

"You miss seeing him around here as much as you used to," Jeter said. "But it was great to hear his voice."

Steinbrenner's statement went on to praise the character and ability of Jeter, comparing him favorably to Gehrig, who died of ALS in 1941, a little more than two years after his final hit. Gehrig was far more prolific as a run producer, but Jeter matched his hit total Wednesday in just 64 fewer plate appearances.

He broke the record with the Yankees comfortably ahead in the division, with a clear path to the playoffs and few pressing team issues. The last few days, then, have played out as a sort of Derek Jeter Appreciation Week for fans and teammates.

During the second delay, of 67 minutes, Girardi sent the regulars home before the game concluded. They appeared in the interview room before leaving, Andy Pettitte, Rodriguez and Jorge Posada sitting at a podium, swapping stories about their teammate and friend.

Pettitte and Posada were second-year professionals in 1992, when Jeter joined their Class A team in Greensboro, N.C., late in the season. Jeter made nine errors in 11 games and hit .243. He was skinny then, and raw as a fielder. But something stood out.

"We were so young and started this run off at such a young age, and you knew that he was special," Pettitte said. "You knew that he carried himself a little bit different than a lot of other guys, a lot of class, a lot of charisma, a lot of confidence for as young as he was."

Rodriguez and Jeter have had a complicated relationship, like Gehrig and Babe Ruth in their day.

But Rodriguez was gracious, calling Jeter the ultimate winner who continues to improve. Jeter is hitting .331.

"I don't think he's ever played any better than he's playing right now, which is awesome," Rodriguez said. "He's running really well, he's playing great defense, he's hitting, he's hitting for power. Where he takes it from now, we're all having fun watching him."

The possibilities were underscored by this oddity: Jeter reached his milestone exactly 24 years after Pete Rose passed Ty Cobb as baseball's career hits leader. Jeter, 35, has more hits than Rose did at the same age. Rose played until age 45 and finished with 4,256 hits.

That chase, if Jeter pursues it, is far off. For now, Jeter said, passing Gehrig is his finest individual accomplishment.

"I can't think of anything else that stands out more so, and I say that because of the person that I was able to pass," Jeter said. "Lou Gehrig, being a former captain and what he stood for, you mention his name to any baseball fan around the country, it means a lot."

Jeter's name holds a similar meaning in the modern game, which he is in no hurry to leave. Jeter is signed through next season and said this week he would keep playing as long as he has fun.

The game is exhilarating now for Jeter, with the Yankees 40 games over .500 and possessing, perhaps, their best chance for a title in years. He has helped carry them with a storm of hits, 188 this season, part of an annual barrage that has set a new standard for the most famous team in sports. ●

A fan holds a sign commemorating Jeter passing Gehrig on the Yankees all-time hits list.
(Richard Perry/The New York Times)

> "We play the game the right way," Jeter said on the podium behind second base, cradling the Commissioner's Trophy. "And we deserve to be standing here."

Back on Top, Yankees Add a 27th Title

By TYLER KEPNER • Published: November 5, 2009

A sliver of time for other teams is an epoch for the Yankees, who define themselves by championships. For eight seasons, they led the majors in victories, payroll and drama. They built a ballpark, created a network and expanded their brand around the globe. But they did not win the World Series.

Now they have done it. There is a 27th jewel in the Yankees' crown and a peaceful, easy feeling across their empire. The Yankees captured their first title since 2000, humbling the defending champion Philadelphia Phillies on Wednesday, 7-3, in Game 6 of the World Series at Yankee Stadium.

Hideki Matsui homered, with his six runs batted in tying a World Series record, and Andy Pettitte ground through five and two-thirds innings for his second victory in five days. Mariano Rivera collected the final five outs, getting Shane Victorino to ground out to second to end it.

"They persevered and they were determined, a lot like the '98 team," General Manager Brian Cashman said, referring to the best Yankees team of modern times. "They had the attitude that nothing was going to stop them. But they had to prove it, and they proved it."

They did it on the eighth anniversary of Rivera's lowest moment, when he blew Game 7 of the 2001 World Series in Arizona. The Yankees lost the World Series again two years later, to Florida, and they did not return until this season, fortifying their roster with free agents around the core of Rivera, Pettitte, Derek Jeter and Jorge Posada.

"We play the game the right way," Jeter said on the podium behind second base, cradling the Commissioner's Trophy. "And we deserve to be standing here."

Pettitte became the second pitcher to win all three clinching games of a postseason. The other was Boston's Derek Lowe in 2004, when

No. 27 for the Yankees. Mariano Rivera, Derek Jeter, and Andy Pettitte, who all won their fifth titles with the Yankees, savor the Series-clinching victory over the Phillies in 2009. (Barton Silverman/The New York Times)

"But this team, they fought and they fought and they fought. They never gave up."
—Hal Steinbrenner

the Yankees lost a three-games-to-none lead to the Red Sox, fumbling away a pennant and plunging into a postseason funk.

Pettitte was gone that autumn, part of a three-year sojourn to his Houston hometown. Otherwise, Pettitte, Rivera, Jeter and Posada have been Yankees since 1995, through dynasty and drought and back to the top. The have each earned five championship rings, one more than Babe Ruth won for the Yankees, who will be honored with a parade in Manhattan on Friday.

It is the seventh championship for the principal owner George Steinbrenner, 79, who was not at Yankee Stadium on Wednesday.

"It's been a while — it's been nine years," said his son, Hal Steinbrenner, the managing general partner. "I just talked to him today. He was a little bit excited and nervous, as we all were. But this team, they fought and they fought and they fought. They never gave up." ●

Jeter takes the field to start Game 6 of the 2009 World Series on November 4, 2009. (Barton Silverman/The New York Times)

"You're talking about from Babe Ruth to Yogi Berra and DiMaggio, Mickey Mantle, all those guys, and none of them have 3,000," Rivera said.

Jeter Reaches Fabled 3,000, and It's a Blast

By TYLER KEPNER • Published: July 9, 2011

The pursuit of a sports milestone can seem like a march to the inevitable. Fans have known for years that barring a catastrophic injury, Derek Jeter would reach 3,000 career hits. The only question was how.

Jeter, the Yankees' captain, answered it Saturday with a performance that ranks among the greatest of his decorated career. He slammed a home run in the third inning for his 3,000th hit, and capped a five-hit day with the go-ahead single in the eighth inning of a 5-4 victory over the Tampa Bay Rays at Yankee Stadium.

Even for Jeter, who dreamed he would be the Yankees shortstop and grew up to lead the team to five championships, the script seemed almost implausible.

"If I would have tried to have written it and given it to someone, I wouldn't have even bought it," Jeter said. "It's just one of those special days."

The 3,000th hit, off a full-count curveball from the left-hander David Price, was Jeter's first over the wall at Yankee Stadium since last June. His five hits matched a career high he had reached only twice before in the regular season, in 2001 and 2005.

Christian Lopez, 23, a fan from Highland Mills, N.Y., caught the ball in the left-field seats and returned it to Jeter, who became the first player with 3,000 hits for the Yankees. Jorge Posada, Jeter's close friend and a teammate for 17 years, wrapped Jeter in a hug at home plate, with reliever Mariano Rivera joining the embrace.

"You're talking about from Babe Ruth to Yogi Berra and DiMaggio, Mickey Mantle, all those guys, and none of them have 3,000," Rivera said. "And then here comes Derek Jeter, for so many years."

Jeter became the 28th player to reach

ᴏN

SportsSunday

SUNDAY, JULY 10, 2011

The New York Times

CAREER DAY

PHOTOGRAPHS BY SUZY ALLMAN FOR THE NEW YORK TIMES

Derek Jeter after hitting a home run Saturday for his 3,000th career hit, which drew a reception of teammates at home plate led by Jorge Posada, below.

By SAM BORDEN

After Homering for 3,000th Hit, Jeter Wins Game With No. 3,003

YANKEES	5
RAYS	4

With one out in the third inning Saturday, space was at a premium on the rail of the Yankees' dugout. Players and staff members crowded shoulder to shoulder, jostling for what they hoped would be the best view of history. Manager Joe Girardi was at one end, arms draped over the railing in his familiar pose; second baseman Robinson Cano was at the other end, a towel across his shoulder and one leg raised on the steps.

Jorge Posada was smack in the middle. Posada is Derek Jeter's best friend on the Yankees, a teammate since 1992, when they were playing Class A ball in Greensboro, N.C. Posada, the longtime Yankees catcher and current designated hitter, had seen so many of Jeter's 2,999 major league hits over the years that he

was not going to miss this one.

When Jeter swung, his shiny black bat meeting a full-count breaking ball from Tampa Bay Rays starter David Price, Posada shot his arms up. He knew, even before the ball had landed in the left-field bleachers, what had happened: Jeter had reached the coveted

3,000-hit mark, the first Yankee to do so, in the most thrilling of fashions.

The Yankees poured onto the field, jumping joyously at home plate as Jeter rounded the bases. With his second hit of the day, in his second at-bat, Jeter — No. 2 — reached the milestone at 2 p.m.

Posada pushed to the front of the mass of players, his smile wide as he wrapped Jeter in a fierce embrace. Mariano Rivera, the third remaining Yankee from the dynasty teams of the 1990s, was right behind Posada, and a receiv-

Continued on Page 3

3,000 hits, but only the second to do so with a home run, after Tampa Bay's Wade Boggs in 1999. Only Ty Cobb, Hank Aaron and Robin Yount joined the club at a younger age than Jeter, who turned 37 on June 26.

That puts Jeter ahead of the pace set by Pete Rose, the career hits leader, who retired at age 45 with 4,256. Jeter is signed for two more years, with a player option for 2014, but he said Thursday that Rose was not on his radar.

"You have to play another five years and get 200 hits to get that extra thousand," Jeter said. "You're talking about a long, long time. You never say never, but it's not something that's on my mind."

Jeter's recent performance offers few hints of Rose's staying power. His .270 average would match last season's figure for the lowest of his career, and he recently spent almost three weeks on the disabled list with a strained calf muscle. Jeter has hit a higher percentage of ground balls (65.3 percent through Friday) than any player in the majors.

Naturally, some of the erosion in his skills can be traced to age, and, perhaps, to the extra wear and tear from roughly a season's worth of games—147—across 30 postseason series. Jeter has also played all his defensive games at shortstop, the most demanding spot on the field besides catcher.

Only one other player reached 3,000 hits while still a regular shortstop: Honus Wagner, in 1914.

"Physically, you have a responsibility that can be difficult, and mentally as well, you have to be in every pitch, every game," Jeter said. "So there's probably a reason why there's not too many guys that have played the position that have had that amount of hits. I take pride in it. This is my job. This is the only thing I've done."

Jeter was a high school shortstop in Kalamazoo, Mich., in 1992, when the Yankees chose him sixth over all in the draft. He advanced to the majors within three years, and by 1996 he was there to stay. Jeter never wanted a day off, he said, for fear that George Steinbrenner, the impatient principal owner, would replace him.

There has never been much danger of that, even after last season, when Jeter's production dipped just as his contract expired. The Yankees gave him a deal worth at least $51 million over three years, but they did so grudgingly, publicly challenging him to explore free agency.

Jeter has said he was angered; he had tried to make it clear he wanted only to play for the Yankees. Meanwhile, he worked to improve in the off-season and in spring training, eliminating his stride in hopes of having more time to react to each pitch. But Jeter abandoned the adjustment soon after the season started and reverted to his old mechanics—without his old results.

The calf injury, however, gave Jeter time to regroup. While recovering at the team's complex in Tampa, Fla., Jeter said, he focused on the basics: staying back in his stance and driving balls up the middle.

"You can get a lot more work in when you don't have to play games," Jeter said. "So I sort of look at it as a blessing in disguise, I hope. I've felt good since I've been back."

However the rest of his career plays out, Jeter—whose 5-for-5 day raised his career average by a point, to .313—will be known most for relentless consistency, for churning out hits at a rate few have matched. Jeter has 10 seasons with at least 190 hits. Only Rose and Cobb, who rank first and second on the career list, have more such seasons.

"I take a lot of pride in going out there every single day and trying to be as consistent as possible," Jeter said. "I think that's probably the most difficult

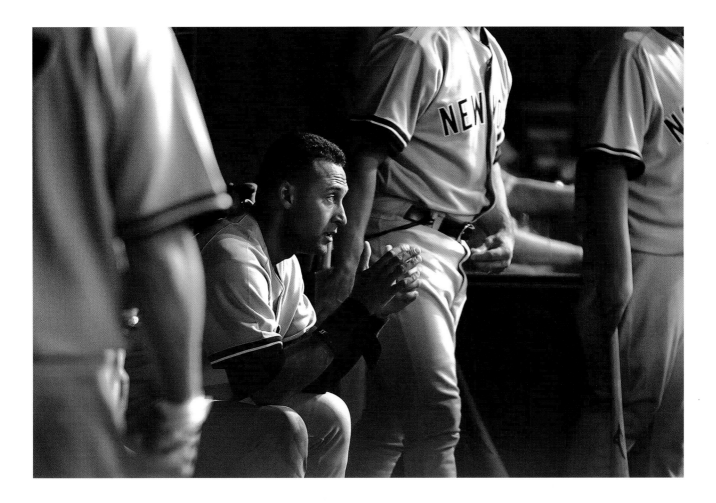

thing to do in our sport. Playing well gets you here. Consistency keeps you here. That's the thing that I've always tried to focus on."

After a game in Cleveland last week, Jeter acknowledged that the scrutiny of his struggles had taken some fun from his chase. But he has seemed more at ease since returning to Yankee Stadium on Thursday, perhaps sensing that his pursuit was nearing an end.

His family and friends have been here, including the former teammates Tino Martinez and Gerald Williams. The scout who signed Jeter, Dick Groch, has been at the ballpark, as have the former Yankees coach Don Zimmer, who works for the Rays, and the former Yankees manager Joe Torre.

"He's just a special kid," Torre said. "I know I keep calling him a kid, but that's what he is."

Jeter was only 20 when he rapped his first hit, a single off the Mariners' Tim Belcher at the Seattle Kingdome on May 30, 1995. It was only appropriate that the 3,000th hit come in the Bronx, where Jeter broke Lou Gehrig's franchise record with 2,722 hits in 2009.

Passing Gehrig was a stirring moment, even if it had little resonance outside Yankee Stadium. With 3,000 hits, Jeter has passed a revered number in the game's history, leaving an indelible mark in style. ●

Jeter in the dugout during a 2007 playoff game against the Indians. (Richard Perry/The New York Times)

The trick is to make summer last as long as possible, to put off reality for another day.

Gray Pinstripes: With Jeter Out, Time's Toll Rises

By TYLER KEPNER • Published: October 14, 2012

It is the one foe every athlete faces, but no athlete can beat. Each knows that the end will come, that age is undefeated in the annals of sports. The trick is to make summer last as long as possible, to put off reality for another day.

The Yankees' best players have done this better than most, with another World Series title at stake this month. Yet bit by bit, and in devastating fashion, the team's aging stars are falling. Derek Jeter, the centerpiece for the last 17 years, is the latest victim, following Mariano Rivera and the since-recovered Andy Pettitte. Jorge Posada retired after last season, and Alex Rodriguez is mired in a deep slump.

The Yankees have lost the first two games of the American League Championship Series to the Detroit Tigers, and Jeter was not there for Sunday's meek 3-0 defeat. He had further tests on the left ankle he fractured in the 12th inning of Game 1, just after midnight. He is done for the postseason, and his next trip, the team said, will be to see a foot and ankle specialist in Charlotte, N.C.

Jeter, who is using crutches and wearing a splint, faces at least three months of recovery at 38. He has company among the aging and ailing.

Five months ago, Rivera, the Yankees' 42-year-old closer, ended his season by tearing a ligament in his right knee while chasing a ball during batting practice at Kansas City. Pettitte, 40, is starting again, but he missed almost half the season after a line drive shattered his ankle in late June.

Posada, the longtime catcher, retired after last season, when he was 40. Rodriguez, 37, is healthy but has had a steady decline in production, finding himself benched for one game this postseason and removed for a pinch-hitter in three others.

"Sometimes, as we all get older, we all feel that we're the same as we used to be," said Yankees Manager Joe Girardi, who turned 48 on Sunday. "It's not really the case. I think, at times, players maybe need a little bit more rest than they would have if they were 25 to 30, and you have to guard against that — and also try to win every game."

That is the Yankees' annual riddle, and to a large extent, they have solved it. Their creaky roster finished the regular season with the most victories in the American League and then eliminated the pesky Baltimore Orioles in a

Jeter is helped off the field after fracturing his ankle in the 12th inning of Game 1 of the 2012 ALDS against the Detroit Tigers. (Barton Silverman/The New York Times)

division series. Jeter's ankle will heal, Rodriguez is signed for five more years, and Rivera and Pettitte have strongly suggested that they hope to continue their careers.

But the day when the Yankees move on from the Jeter era is increasingly coming into focus, and the transition can be painful to witness. On Saturday, Jeter dived to his left for a grounder, a play he has made countless times before. But this time, he could not get up from the dirt, his ankle having finally given out after sustaining a bone bruise in September and taking a barrage of foul balls off it in the Baltimore series.

"This is a tough story for baseball — what he has done in the postseason, what he means to the Yankees, what he means to baseball in general," Tigers Manager Jim Leyland said, adding later, "It's sad, really."

On Sunday, the Yankees played their first postseason game without either Jeter or Rivera on the active roster since the final game of the 1981 World Series, their last postseason appearance before returning in 1995. They had replaced Rivera with Rafael Soriano, who had a terrific season. But Soriano was largely on the roster for that purpose, a former All-Star signed as a possible successor to Rivera.

Jeter's replacement is Jayson Nix, a 30-year-old who has played for five teams and has a .214 career average. Nix said Jeter sent him a text message Sunday.

"It just said good luck, he believes in me, and go get 'em," Nix said.

That is more than Jeter was saying in the training room after the injury. Joe Torre, who managed Jeter for 12 years with the Yankees and now works as an executive in the commissioner's office, was there when the team doctor gave Jeter

Jeter addressed fans during a pregame tribute to George Steinbrenner and Bob Sheppard at Yankee Stadium in July 2010. (Uli Seit/The New York Times)

"Losing Derek, especially in the postseason, it stinks," reliever Dave Robertson said. "It's the last guy you want to see go down."

the diagnosis. According to Torre, Jeter said nothing. Torre said he had never seen Jeter so down.

"The fact that he was hurt is one thing, and also the fact that he knows that he can't be there for them to play," Torre said. "It sounds hokey, but it's true. He's indestructible. It's one of those things; you never even question whether he stumbles and falls if he's going to play."

Jeter has sustained one other serious injury, dislocating his shoulder on opening night in 2003 on a collision with a catcher at third base in Toronto. That night, before he had even gotten up off the ground, Jeter told Torre he would play the next day. He missed six weeks.

After this injury, Jeter seemed to grasp the severity instantly. On the field, he did not plead with Girardi for playing time. He asked only for his dignity.

"Jeet has always been as tough as a player as I've ever been around, and that's what he showed, was toughness," Girardi said. "I mean, even when I went to the field and I was going to carry him in, he said, 'No — do not carry me.' That is the kind of guy he is."

Jeter experienced a renaissance this season, leading the major leagues in hits, with 216, while batting .316. He came to bat 740 times, the most in the majors, and in Game 1 on Saturday, he collected his 200th career postseason hit — 72 more than any other

player. The Yankees owe him $20 million for the next two seasons, or $25 million if Jeter exercises his player option for 2014.

He has often said that he will play as long as he enjoys himself, a sentiment that had never been in doubt, especially on the October stage. His teammate Mark Teixeira said he felt terrible that the injury occurred in the playoffs, not because it hurt the Yankees' chances, but because Jeter lived for these moments.

"We probably feel worse for him than anyone else who could go out," Teixeira said.

The Yankees move on to Detroit now, without their leader. In Game 3 they must face the Tigers' ace, Justin Verlander, with a slumbering offense and a growing sense of doom.

"Losing Derek, especially in the postseason, it stinks," reliever Dave Robertson said. "It's the last guy you want to see go down. There's nothing we can do about it now. All we can do is push forward." ●

1994 **2004** **2014**

CAPTAIN'S LOG

The all-time Yankees hits leader's year-by-year totals:

Year	Hits
1995	12
1996	183
1997	190
1998	203
1999	219
2000	201
2001	191
2002	191
2003	156
2004	188
2005	202
2006	214
2007	206
2008	179
2009	212
2010	179
2011	162
2012	216
2013	12
2014	149

TOTAL: 3465

I told you guys. One more year. Smile. No long conversation.

Jeter's Retirement Announcement Hits the Right Note

By GEORGER VECSEY • Published: February 12, 2014

This retirement is so Derek Jeter. So smooth, so efficient, so convenient for all concerned.

It's kind of like a fielder flitting through the tall weeds of disaster and finding a wayward baseball and flipping it homeward, thereby saving his side from a mess of trouble. That would be so Derek Jeter. Just look up Giambi, Jeremy.

So is announcing his retirement just before teammates and fans and "you guys"—the old Michael Jordan "you guys"—arrive at his Florida base in Tampa. He beat everybody to the punch, just as he has done since he showed up in the 1995 season.

Jeter is confining the tensions—No-Drama Derek—for this season, making sure he will not be a distraction. His stated position on his health has always been "I'm fine"—even when he might have had a broken bone or something. Now he can conduct his own private little batter-pitcher duel with old age itself, try to get his rebelling body back to its old level of performance. And if not, he has given the Yankees, given everybody, a limit.

I told you guys. One more year. Smile. No long conversation.

The Yankees can plan, he can plan. Some great players, like Ted Williams and Stan Musial, had one more great hitting season left around the age of 40. True, they were not trying to be the highly effective shortstop that Jeter has been. All the details will take care of themselves. This makes it clear. One more time around.

Jeter has known how to handle himself since his arrival with the Yankees. He is the beneficiary of a tight family unit—Charles Jeter, an addiction counselor; Dorothy Jeter, an accountant; and his sister, Sharlee, five years younger. There is every indication that all three have expected him not to be a jerk, in public or in private. One would wish internal controls like his for many other athletes who enter public life and have no clue how to act.

He did not smirk or pout when the Yankees reverted to older shortstops after he had filled

Jeter and Alfonso Soriano celebrate a Yankees win. (Barton Silverman/The New York Times)

Yankee Who Lived a Dream Says It's Near End

TYLER KEPNER

ON BASEBALL

The greatest compliment we can give Derek Jeter, as he prepares to leave the grandest stage in baseball, is that he never let us down. He has made thousands of outs and hundreds of errors and finished most of his seasons without a championship. Yet he never disappointed us.

This is no small feat for the modern athlete, in an age of endless traps and temptations.

From cheating to preening to taunting — even to defensible acts, like fleeing to a new team in free agency — the hero, almost invariably, breaks our heart

sometime. Not Jeter.

He grew up beside a baseball diamond in Kalamazoo, Mich., dreaming of playing shortstop for the Yankees, and that is what he has done. He has never played another position, never been anything but No. 2 for the Yankees. But this season, he announced Wednesday, will be his last.

"The one thing I always said to myself was that when baseball started to feel more like a job, it would be time to move forward," Jeter said in a statement on Facebook, adding later: "I could not be more sure. I know it in my heart. The 2014 season will be my last year playing profecsional baseball."

When Jeter played his first

game at the old Yankee Stadium, on June 2, 1995, the announced crowd was 16,959. By 2008, when he closed the ballpark with a speech to the fans, the average attendance topped 53,000. For the Yankees, Jeter was the right player at the right time, a model of stability and the embodiment of their ideals.

Jeter has compiled 3,316 hits (10th on baseball's career list), winning five championships while making more than $250 million in salary. But his impact has always been greater than his numbers.

When Jeter joined the organization, as a high schooler drafted sixth over all in 1992, the Yankees

Continued on Page B21

in for a few games during the 1995 season. Think the Yankees would have beaten Seattle in that great series if the club had seen what fans and writers saw?

Jeter has done something more than help win seven pennants and five World Series. He helped turn the Yankees into a team that Mets fans, Red Sox fans, can respect (at least some of them; there are always hardheads). He and his contemporaries—Bernie Williams, Jorge Posada, Mariano Rivera and Andy Pettitte, as well as Joe Torre (whom Jeter calls Mr. T) and Joe Girardi— took some of the starch and bluster and gloom and doom out of the old Yankee ways.

As the captain, Jeter did it without sacrificing his privacy. Some New York players manage to be surprisingly open, and therefore vulnerable, in the daily locker-room soap opera. Jeter was much more private. Who knows his taste in politics or music or books? When other people got into trouble or said stupid things, you had to read Jeter's chosen words the way one reads the Mona Lisa's smile.

In 2009, while Alex Rodriguez was going through one of his many frolics over performance-enhancing drugs, Jeter gave a measured comment. "One thing that irritates me is that this was the steroid era," he said. "I don't know how many people tested positive, but everybody wasn't doing it." I've come to think that was the most candid thing I ever heard him say.

Now Jeter begins the orderly process of going out the right way. Just the other day, eager for baseball, I worked up a little essay on Jeter that asked, "Is it too much to ask that Derek Jeter be healthy and productive for one more season, clapping his hands at second base and retiring knuckleheads?" I was thinking of his double into the corner that started the rally against Pedro Martinez in 2003.

This final season could go a lot of different ways for Derek Jeter, but he will conduct it the right way. ●

"He has given the Yankees, given everybody, a limit." (Barton Silverman/The New York Times)

Jeter has built a career on grit and hustle, on an inside-out swing and a jump throw to first from deep in the hole

The Book on Jeter

By DOUG GLANVILLE • Published: February 14, 2014

Every major league player is deeded real estate in the book of baseball. Some may be granted only one word, others a paragraph. And then there is Derek Jeter, who is closing out, in a masterly way, one of the great chapters in baseball's history.

It is rare when you can craft both the beginning and end of your entry and also guide the pen in between. The serendipity that marks a life in the game can add pages of unforeseen horror (or romance) to your story. The wayward hand of the larger forces in baseball can act like a toddler's first dance with a crayon. Wantonly scribbling out previous work, recklessly writing outside the lines without control.

But a major league player has a magic pen, too. In Jeter's letter to the fans, he expressed a common player belief that this game was a dream, the domain of the supernatural and unexplainable, enduring against all odds. So you tap your dreams, and accept that every once in a while they will be interrupted by a trip to the disabled list or a subpar season. Yet Jeter lived the daily dream of being an exceptional player with an exceptional organization behind him, and he became one of the best of baseball's dream.

Jeter has built a career on grit and hustle, on an inside-out swing and a jump throw to first from deep in the hole. The ice water in his veins enabled him to expect victory in the most dire circumstances, and doubled as an antidote to the sometimes venomous scrutiny that comes with playing in New York.

Jeter has always been daring and fearless, and it takes a lot of courage to pre-empt the inevitable physical decline of a professional baseball player and do what he did this week: declare a self-imposed deadline and submit, finally, to baseball's history book. The game's actuarial tables don't generally put a 40-year-old shortstop in the starting lineup on Opening Day for any contender, so he already enters this season as an anomaly.

Yet no player can completely control the ending. Happenstance is one of baseball's great gifts and curses. When you are playing 162 games in a season, nearly every single day, anything can happen.

Jeter never gave up until he knew beyond a shadow of a doubt that it was over, and even then, he winked. He is pragmatic and knows the risk of entering a season at this stage in his career without a plan: it's an invitation to chaos. There would be the inevitable questions about a slow bat or an unhealed ankle, the distractions

Jeter shows the ball to the umpire as he makes his case. (Barton Silverman/The New York Times)

and self-doubts that come with a slump at 40 versus a slump at 25.

In many ways, Jeter's declaration not only provided parameters for himself, it spared his teammates and his manager. They will not have to explain his future struggles, they will not have to consider joining a conversation that suggests he think about retirement.

Truth is, he does not know how this year will unfold. We can imagine the impossible—like a standing ovation in his honor at Fenway Park or a game-winning home run in Game 7 of the World Series—because all along he played for something bigger than rivalry and organizational pride. Those priorities earn the respect of anyone who loves the game and cares about its future. Jeter transcended tried-and-true constructs, and it would be fitting if his transition from the game were transcendent.

But even though Jeter's baseball legacy will be there for all time, the world changes, and how that legacy is interpreted will change with it. This is what is so hard. Even if we end on our terms, we still can't know how we will be remembered.

We hope there is something immutable about our effort. That we are somehow timeless and forever. But we have to wait and see, and clarity still might not come in our lifetime. As Jeter stated in his letter to his fans, "Now it is time for a new chapter. I have new dreams and aspirations, and I want new challenges."

His greatest challenge may be those first steps without the pinstripes, without the packed stadium, without the opponent 60 feet 6 inches away. It might arise while he's sitting on the couch, opening up baseball's history and seeing his entry complete, with nothing more to be added.

But the good news, as baseball turns to the next chapter, is that it's a game that looks forward and backward equally, and something tells me that Derek Jeter will be that rarity who will find a way to travel through time and stand in both the past and in the future. ●

"He became one of the best of baseball's dream." (Both photos: Barton Silverman/The New York Times)

"I'm always going to tell you I'm fine," he said with a sheepish grin. "This year, I mean it."

Jeter Savoring His Last Season but Not Letting It Distract Him

By DAVID WALDSTEIN • Published: February 20, 2014

TAMPA, Fla.—In the ninth inning of the penultimate game at the old Yankee Stadium in 2008, Derek Jeter was trying to absorb every aspect of the final moments at the sacred grounds. He knew there would be only a few more at-bats there, and he wanted to soak them up.

But shortly after he looked around at the cheering fans and their signs, perhaps a glance at the classic facade and the spots in the stands where he had hit postseason home runs, he was snapped out of his reverie by a pitch from Baltimore Orioles reliever Jim Miller—now a Yankee—that hit him on the wrist.

"I decided I wasn't going to do that again," he said.

For all his talk about soaking in his final year in baseball, Jeter used that story to make a point: Smelling the roses is fine, but Jeter said he could not be distracted from the work needed to get ready for his final season.

So on the first day of full-squad workouts for the 2014 Yankees, a thinner Jeter noticed the larger-than-normal crowd with their adoring signs and photographs of him. He waved to a few of them from the batting cage, and he had his usual laughs with teammates and coaches on the field. But he also had his job to take care of, and, according to Manager Joe Girardi, it was the best day he had seen Jeter have physically in well over a year.

"I would say last year at times, just going through what you might consider everyday activity—a jog, running the bases—you would notice it," Girardi said of Jeter's 2013 limp. "Today I noticed nothing. To me, it looked like he never got hurt."

For many Yankee fans saddened by the news that this will be Jeter's final season, those are encouraging words. Girardi watched along with 1,338 fans and dozens of members of the news media, most of whom were representing Japanese outlets interested in Masahiro Tanaka, Ichiro Suzuki and the spring training guest instructor Hideki Matsui.

Girardi watched as Jeter took easy ground balls for about 15 minutes along with the other infielders. Then Jeter stepped back and caught hard grounders, firing across the infield to first base. That was followed by a round of batting

Jeter hits a grounder against the Pirates' Charlie Morton in a mid-May game. (Barton Silverman/The New York Times)

practice—including tracking live pitches from Preston Claiborne—and finally some running. Earlier, he hit in the indoor cages.

Throughout the day Jeter did not move gingerly or exhibit any limp or false steps. He gave no indication that he was not healthy, now 16 months removed from surgery on his broken ankle.

Jeter concurred with Girardi's assessment, saying there was no comparison with last year. A year ago, Jeter removed the protective boot in early January and never had a chance to do the proper conditioning for the rest of his body. This year, he did.

Then again, a year ago he claimed he felt fine as well.

"I'm always going to tell you I'm fine," he said with a sheepish grin. "This year, I mean it."

To take pressure off his legs and move better throughout the season, Jeter said he had lost roughly six pounds through extra conditioning and a better diet. He hopes to remain at that weight all year.

For the past 10 years, Jeter said, he has played at 199 pounds and almost never deviated from that. So consistent was his weight through the past decade that before he stepped on the scale, the trainer Steve Donohue would announce, "199."

But this year, Jeter said he was 193 or 194 pounds.

Girardi said not to expect Jeter to play in the first couple of spring training games, but aside from that he did not envision any restrictions. The goal is for Jeter to get 60 at-bats in spring training and to be ready to play regularly throughout the season.

Perhaps because of Jeter's impending retirement, or maybe because of the Japanese stars, Girardi said he had noticed more buzz in the stands and from the news media for the first workout. He also noted that the new players participating in their first workouts as Yankees, including Jacoby Ellsbury and Carlos Beltran, might have been a factor as well.

"I believe we had a very good off-season," Girardi said, and added, "I like what I see." ●

Above: Jeter squares one up. Opposite: Jeter congratulates Brett Gardner on a run scored. (Both photos: Barton Silverman/The New York Times)

"It's not only a credit to him; it's a credit
our guy and this guy is going to play

With 2,583 Games at One Position, Derek Jeter Reaches Another Milestone

By DAVID WALDSTEIN • Published: May 23, 2014

CHICAGO—It seems that barely a day goes by without Derek Jeter breaking a record or passing a milestone.

Most of the statistics relate to his offense. For instance, Jeter recently passed Paul Molitor for eighth place on the career hits list, and on Friday night, he passed Lou Gehrig for second on the Yankees' runs-scored list with 1,889.

Jeter, however, also reached a defensive milestone of sorts on Friday, one that speaks to his remarkable longevity.

With the Yankees facing the Chicago White Sox, Jeter was in the lineup for his 2,583rd game at shortstop, putting him in a tie for second among all shortstops with Luis Aparicio, a White Sox great who was an integral part of their 1959 pennant-winning team. Only Omar Vizquel has played more games (2,709) at the position, one of the most demanding in baseball.

"Aparicio!" Jeter exclaimed after the game, a 6-5 Yankees loss. "Everyone knows how great he is. I guess it's ironic that we're here. It's hard to believe when you think about the history of the game and there is only one guy who has played more games.

"It's something I'm proud of. I take pride in doing my job and being available to play every day. To have your name in the company of someone like him is pretty special."

White Sox Manager Robin Ventura, who played alongside Jeter in 2002 and 2003 as a Yankee, said before the game: "It's pretty amazing, to do it at that position. That's the hardest position to play other than catcher."

Even more remarkable: When Jeter passes Aparicio, who also played for the Baltimore Orioles and the Boston Red Sox, he will become the only player to have made that many appearances at one infield position without ever playing another defensive position. (Vizquel played a little third base, some second base and even left and right field.)

Whatever the reason—whether his own stubbornness and pride or the Yankees' never

to the Yankees that they decided this is here for a long time," Girardi said.

seeing the need to ask him to move to a different position—Jeter has remained strictly a shortstop for 20 seasons.

"For him to be able to stay there his whole career says a lot," Ventura said. "It's kind of incredible."

At times, fans and analysts wondered if Jeter would end up in left field, at third base or at first. Perhaps he would even be permanently relegated to designated hitter.

But such a move never happened, and it does not appear as if it will. Jeter, who has said he will retire after the season, has played 40 games this year, and only one as D.H.

Jeter, who played his 2,642nd game over all on Friday, went 2 for 4 to raise his batting average this season to .268. He now has 3,358 hits—ninth on the career list.

Jeter will turn 40 on June 26. According to Baseball Prospectus, only three regular shortstops (those with more than 400 appearances) have played at that age: Vizquel, with the 2007 San Francisco Giants; Honus Wagner, with the 1914 Pittsburgh Pirates; and Luke Appling, with the 1947 White Sox.

Joe Girardi, who has managed the Yankees since 2008, when Jeter was 33, said he had never been part of a discussion about changing Jeter's position.

He knows that Jeter is not the best shortstop in baseball and that, at his age and coming off a broken ankle, Jeter is probably at the bottom of the list in terms of mobility. Still, Jeter charges balls well, and anything hit to him is about as close to a guaranteed out as there is.

So far, Girardi has said, the Yankees do not feel that Jeter has hurt them in the field. Asked how Jeter

had managed to stay at such a tricky position for 20 years, Girardi said it came down to hard work.

"It's his effort," Girardi said before the game. "The winters and during the years taking care of his body; taking care of himself at night. You don't read about Derek in places at 2 and 3 in the morning. That's not who he is. He understands he has a responsibility to the team, and he takes care of himself."

Ventura recalled the first time he saw Jeter play, in 1996, when Jeter was in his first full major league season and Ventura was a third baseman for the White Sox. The White Sox also had a young player named Lyle Mouton, who came up in the Yankees' farm system and played with Jeter in the minor leagues.

"He told us to watch this kid," Ventura said. "He said he could play. I remember thinking, 'Yeah, he is good.' You don't know that it's going to turn into all this, but you could see he could play."

Jeter, despite his grit, his sure-handedness and his ability to throw while jumping, was never considered among the best fielders in the game. It was more his ability to hit, combined with his consistency, his reputation as a winner and, later, his iconic status, that kept him a shortstop with the Yankees.

"It's not only a credit to him; it's a credit to the Yankees that they decided this is our guy and this guy is going to play here for a long time," Girardi said. "They signed him to a major long-term contract and then signed him to another one. So I think it's a credit to both groups because Derek lived up to the long-term contract and the Yankees rewarded him. It's amazing what he's done in his career. The consistency, still being able to play shortstop—it's really amazing." ●

"He just wanted to thank us," Trout said. "You know, we should be thanking him."

M.L.B. All-Star Game 2014: Derek Jeter Nabs 2 Hits in A.L. Victory

By TYLER KEPNER • Published: July 16, 2014

MINNEAPOLIS—In the final act of his final All-Star Game, Derek Jeter did something that was quintessentially him. Asked about his first at-bat here on Tuesday, and Adam Wainwright's in-game acknowledgment that he had deliberately given him a good pitch to hit, Jeter tried humor to defuse a bubbling controversy.

After beginning with a serious assessment of Wainwright's pitches, Jeter pivoted suddenly. "I don't know, man," he said, to laughter. "If he grooved it, thank you. You've still got to hit it. I appreciate that, if that's what he did."

Jeter ripped a leadoff double to the right-field corner off Wainwright, then scored as part of a three-run inning to help lift the American League to a 5-3 victory over the National League at Target Field. For the 12th year in a row, the winning league gets home-field advantage in the World Series.

Jeter finished his All-Star Game career with a .481 average (13 for 27) after a single off Alfredo Simon in the third. He went back to shortstop for the top of the fourth, but before Chris Sale's first pitch, Alexei Ramirez took the field to replace Jeter at short.

Jeter pointed to the N.L. dugout as he left the diamond, pausing before the baseline and then stepping over it, like Burt Lancaster in "Field of Dreams," crossing a threshold and knowing he could not return. That was the end of his All-Star Game career.

With "New York, New York" playing over the loudspeakers, and his parents cheering on the scoreboard, Jeter walked the length of the first base dugout, exchanging handshakes and hugs with each of the players and coaches. He returned to the field for another ovation, tipping his cap—a garish All-Star Game-only version, with a white panel in the front—to the crowd.

Mike Trout and Jeter spoke admiringly of each other after the victory, and Trout was asked about Jeter's pregame message to the team. Jeter told the players the experience goes quickly, and urged them to enjoy every minute.

"He just wanted to thank us," Trout said. "You know, we should be thanking him." ●

Jeter waves to the crowd after being removed in the 4th inning of the 2014 All-Star Game. (AP Photo/Jeff Roberson)

"I got to second base, and I told him, 'It's been an honor playing with you, a privilege,'" said Royals left fielder Alex Gordon. "I think everybody would say that if they ran into him."

Celebrating Glory, With Little Hope to Add to It

By TYLER KEPNER • Published: September 7, 2014

Michael Jordan finished his Chicago Bulls career by making a shot that clinched an N.B.A. championship. Jordan did not quit for good right then, but popular mythology freezes him forever as a winner, his final moment unfolding like a dream.

Derek Jeter has carried Jordan's banner in baseball, in the logo he wears on his cleats and the steely competitiveness of his play. On Sunday, after Jordan's surprise appearance at the Yankees' pregame ceremony to honor their retiring captain, Jeter called Jordan the older brother he never had.

"He constantly reminds me that he has six and I have five," Jeter said, referring to championship rings, an edge Jordan will hold on him forever.

The final Yankees team of the Jeter era is just not up to it. Its offense is weak, and its top pitchers are hurt.

C. C. Sabathia gallantly escorted Jeter's sister, Sharlee, and nephew, Jalen, onto the field for the ceremony, but his knee has not allowed him to pitch since May. Another ace, Masahiro Tanaka, is out with elbow trouble.

So on Jeter's big day, it was a wobbly rookie, Shane Greene, who took the ball in the pivotal game — in truth, they are all pivotal now — and lost to the Kansas City Royals. The Royals have not reached the postseason since Jeter was in sixth grade, but they shut out the Yankees twice in three games.

They did it Sunday despite their open admiration, even awe, for their opponent. The Royals watched the ceremony for Jeter from the top step of their dugout and then stepped onto the field for a better view during Jeter's speech. Some of them took photos and videos with their phones.

"We didn't discuss it," said Alex Gordon, the Royals' left fielder. "Everybody just had respect for him."

The Yankees removed the Royals' flag — and the flag of every other major league team

Fans file in to Yankee Stadium on Derek Jeter Day, Sept. 7, 2014. (Barton Silverman/The New York Times)

— from atop Yankee Stadium, ringing their imperial palace with Jeter flags. His No. 2 flapped overhead while adorning the Yankees' sleeves and caps down below, as it will for the rest of the season.

If this all seems a bit much, the players would never complain. Jeter is this generation's idol, for his grace and his comportment and, significantly, his skill in navigating the temptations all players face without public missteps. Jordan touched on this in his comments after the ceremony.

"In this era, very few people take the time to say 'what if' before they make a decision," Jordan said. "And he's done that, and he's made the right decision each and every time."

Jeter has surely made some bad decisions — he is human, despite all the pomp — but none that would tarnish his crown as benevolent king of the game. The commissioner-elect, Rob Manfred, was among the guests to honor him on Sunday. The outgoing commissioner, Bud Selig, hinted over the weekend that Jeter would soon receive his special achievement award.

"I got to second base, and I told him, 'It's been an honor playing with you, a privilege,'" Gordon said. "I think everybody would say that if they ran into him."

Gordon presumably said that in the third inning Sunday, on his way to scoring the Royals' second run in a 2-0 victory. Jeter had an infield single, a walk, a strikeout and a groundout. His teammates managed just three other singles and never set foot on third base.

Manager Joe Girardi has batted Jeter first or second all season. He has few other appealing options and still trusts Jeter in the clutch. This is how it will end for Jeter — at the top of the order and, in his 20-year career, in no place on the field other than shortstop.

That is truly remarkable historically, but unblemished records and round-number symmetry are part of the mystique of the Yankees' recent past. You half expected Manfred to step to the podium and decree the Yankees winners of the 1997 World Series, just to give them five in a row for that era, to match Yogi Berra's best run.

Look at Jeter's career hit total in the postseason: an even 200 for the man who wears No. 2. (Mariano Rivera, who wore No. 42 and earned 42 postseason saves, could relate.) Unless the Yankees leap three teams in the wild-card race, those playoff statistics will never change.

That would also mean that the final image of Jeter in October would be that grisly play at shortstop against Detroit in 2012, when Jeter's ankle snapped as he dived for a bouncer to his left.

He walked off his favorite stage — "Do not carry me," he told Girardi that night, through the pain — but quite likely, that was the end.

"We're still in a position, if we win our games, we'll be all right," Jeter said after Sunday's loss. He was bending the math to gain control of a race others dictate.

In theory, the Yankees could win out and still not reach the playoffs. Jeter's friends sense how badly he wants to go out a winner, to at least have a chance at that sixth ring. Jorge Posada said he had tried to encourage Jeter.

"I told him, 'September's always been a good month for you, so go out there and do what you do and help the team get to where it needs to be,'" Posada said. "It's tough. I feel for him."

Jeter, of course, has experienced his share of winning. He has collected more championships in his career than 22 other franchises have in their existence. He has lived his career to the fullest, honoring his talents and respecting the game, leaving a powerful legacy on the field and off. ●

The fans show Jeter their appreciation as he heads to the plate. (Barton Silverman/The New York Times)

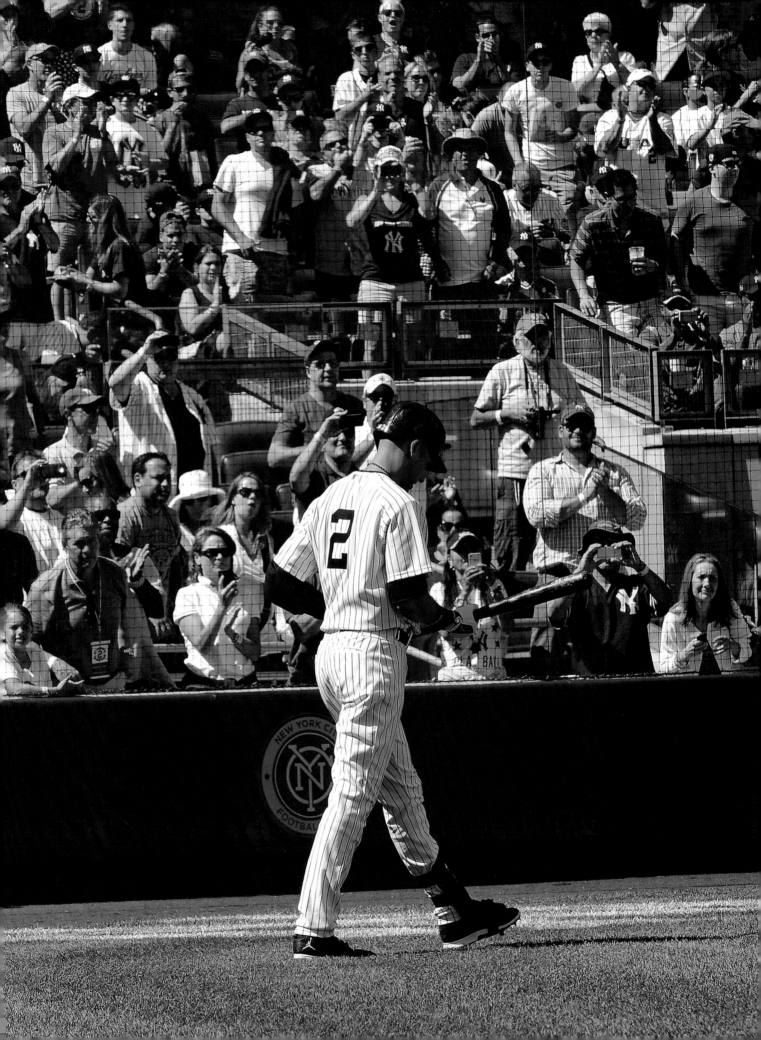

In Enemy Territory, a Farewell

Derek Jeter Plays Final Game at Fenway Park

By TYLER KEPNER • Published: September 28, 2014

BOSTON — Sunlight bathed the field when Derek Jeter came to bat Sunday for the last time in the major leagues. Only the home plate area, from which Jeter stared down Boston starter Clay Buchholz, was in shadows.

Jeter took a strike and a ball, smacked a ball foul and then beat a 93-mile-an-hour fastball off the plate.

The ball hung in the air for three seconds. The third baseman leapt for it and tipped it with his bare hand. The ball fell to the Fenway Park grass as Jeter raced through first base, with no throw. This was his 3,465th and final hit, a figure surpassed by only five others in history.

Jeter already had his magic moment on Thursday, in his Yankee Stadium finale, when he played shortstop for the last time and singled home the winning run in the bottom of the ninth. He could have sat out this series, like the Red Sox great Ted Williams, who homered in his last at-bat at Fenway, in 1960, and did not even travel to New York to wrap up the year.

But Jeter said he owed it to the fans here, and the teams' rivalry, to make an appearance.

He went 1 for 2 on Saturday and again on Sunday, each hit an infield single that found its way to a Boston rookie named Garin Cecchini.

Cecchini was barely a year old when the Yankees drafted Jeter in 1992. He grew up in Louisiana, as a shortstop, and Jeter was his favorite player. He wears No. 70, the digits of a player who still must prove himself. It happens to be the number the Yankees assigned Jeter in spring training the year before he made the majors.

"He's a guy you respect and you kind of want to idolize because everyone liked him," Cecchini said. "And he was a winner. He's won a lot of games, won championships. That's all you want to be recognized as in this sport: a winner."

The Yankees won five titles with Jeter, and the Red Sox won three during his career. This season, neither team made the playoffs. Given the standings, and the gripping finale in the Bronx, the weekend had the feeling of a bonus track on a masterpiece album, the way the Beatles tacked "Her Majesty," a brief aside,

Comes With a Warm Embrace.

on to the soaring medley that otherwise closed out "Abbey Road."

Few of the game's grand figures go out in style. Mickey Mantle — 46 years ago to the day, also at Fenway Park — popped out to shortstop in the first inning and never played again. Yogi Berra finished with a fielder's choice groundout for the Mets in 1965. Lou Gehrig and Babe Ruth went hitless in their final games, in the 1930s.

Jeter's last hit did not go far, but it nudged his career average up a point, to .310, where it will sit forever. He finished with 1,923 runs scored — an evocative number in the history of the Yankees, who won their first title in 1923 — and nobody ever started more games at shortstop than Jeter's 2,660.

With two hits on Sunday, Jeter could have tied Ty Cobb's record for most seasons of 150 hits, with 18. Manager Joe Girardi told him of the possibility on Sunday morning, he said, believing it was his obligation. Jeter was not swayed. His plan was to bat twice and take the results, whatever they were.

"I never played the game for numbers," he said. "So why start now?"

Jeter arrived in the visitors' clubhouse at 10:50 a.m., coming in on the team bus and chatting along the concourse with Tim Wakefield, a former Red Sox knuckleballer whom he faced more than any other pitcher. He passed souvenir stands that sold T-shirts and caps and pink foam fingers commemorating his career. He was not an enemy this weekend.

He dressed in his usual Fenway locker, the last in a row of four green stalls, closest to the tunnel leading to the field. He laughed with Brett Gardner and Chris Young and spoke with Jeff Idelson, the president of the Hall of Fame. He came across the young son of the Yankees' pitching coach, Larry Rothschild, patting him on the shoulder and offering his standard greeting: "What's up, buddy?"

Jeter smiled a lot during batting practice, the fans practically spilling onto the dirt track behind the cage, holding signs for him. Spike Lee and Joe Torre looked on. Jeter joined his teammates in the outfield for a silly footrace between two plodders, Mark Teixeira and Brian McCann. Teixeira won.

Soon enough came the ceremony on the field, featuring Boston sports greats like Carl Yastrzemski and Bobby Orr. Pete Frates, the former Boston College baseball captain who inspired the A.L.S. Ice Bucket Challenge, was there, too, and a singer from "The Voice" serenaded Jeter with Aretha Franklin's "Respect."

The gifts were modest — a pair of duck boots, a base with his number on it, a signed "RE2PECT" plate from the scoreboard, a check to his foundation — and the cheers from the fans heartfelt. Jeter had been a worthy rival. ●

Jeter is mobbed by teammates after hitting a walk-off single in the Captain's final game at Yankee Stadium, on Thursday, September 25, 2014. (Michelle V. Agins/The New York Times)